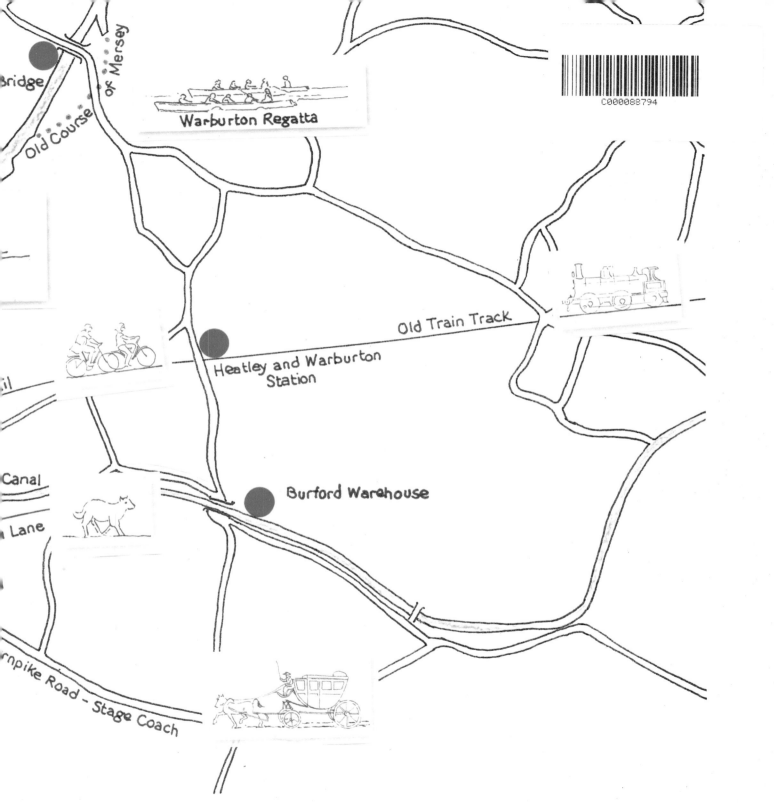

Bridge

Old Course of Mersey

Warburton Regatta

Old Train Track

Heatley and Warburton Station

Canal

Lane

Burford Warehouse

Turnpike Road - Stage Coach

To Su & Eileen

THE WHEELS
AND
THE WATER

© Alan Williams & Alan Taylor

Published by The Leckonby Press.   2013
Leckonby Cottage,
11A Whitbarrow Road, Lymm, Cheshire UK WA13 9AG
Email alanlymm@gmail.com

ISBN 978-0-9927649-0-6

British Library Cataloguing-in-Publication Data
A catalogue record for this book is available from the British Library.

While every effort has been made to ensure the accuracy and quality of information in this publication, the Publisher accepts no responsibility for the subsequent use of this information or any errors or omissions that it may contain, or for any misunderstanding arising from it.

FRONT COVER: Manchester Ship Canal at Statham (1957) *Alan Taylor*
BACK COVER :   Eagle Brow, Lymm Village Centre (1958)   *Alan Taylor*
TITLE PAGE: The Locomotive "Lymm " 1890s *Lymm History Society*

THE WHEELS
AND
THE WATER

*The story of Lymm's
journey through the
transport revolution*

ALAN WILLIAMS & ALAN TAYLOR

The Leckonby Press

Contents

Introduction

HISTORY ON THE DOORSTEP   8

LYMM'S TRANSPORT TIMELINE   9

The Age of Horsepower

THE ENGINE THAT DROVE THE VILLAGE   10

The Most Extraordinary Thing

THE STORY OF THE DUKE OF BRIDGEWATER'S CANAL   18

HISTORIC TRANSPORT DAY ON THE CANAL   30

THE FUSTIAN CUTTERS OF LYMM   36

LIFE AT A CANAL WAREHOUSE   38

THE LYMM MYSTERY   39

Turnpikes and Toll Bridges

FROM CART-TRACKS TO HIGHWAYS   40

The Steam Era

RAILWAY MANIA REACHES LYMM   48

THE MERSEY & IRWELL REGATTA AT WARBURTON   58

BOYHOOD MEMORIES OF HEATLEY & WARBURTON STATION   60

WHAT HAPPENED NEXT AT HEATLEY & WARBURTON STATION   62

A REAL EL DORADO   63

HISTORIC TRANSPORT DAY ON THE RAILS   64

Ships Across the Fields

THE MANCHESTER SHIP CANAL   66

THE LOCOMOTIVE LYMM   77

Pedalling History

A QUIET REVOLUTION FOR THE WORKING MAN AND WOMAN   78

HISTORIC TRANSPORT DAY BY BICYCLE   83

A TRIP FROM MANCHESTER TO LYMM   84

THE INVASION OF ROSTHERNE   86

That Intolerable Nuisance

THE COMING OF THE MOTOR CAR   88

HISTORIC TRANSPORT DAY ON THE ROAD   100

THE SELF-PROPELLED TRAFFIC ASSOCIATION   106

CATCHING THE BUS   108

MY FIRST CAR   110

PUTTING THE SPORT IN TRANSPORT   113

ONE MAN'S JOURNEY FROM BY-WAY TO HIGHWAY   114

Back to the Future

A VILLAGE AT THE CROSSROADS   116

POPLAR TRANSPORT HERITAGE CENTRE   118

ACKNOWLEDGEMENTS, BIBLIOGRAPHY   121

PICTURE CREDITS   122

ABOUT THE AUTHORS, THE BIG PICTURE   123

Introduction

HISTORY ON THE DOORSTEP

It is something of a cliché to say that we often fail to see and appreciate what we have on our own doorstep. Our family have been lucky enough to live next to the canal in Lymm for twenty years. We enjoy taking our visitors out for a walk on the towpath but their questions about when and why the canal was built are met with my mumbled and uncertain response. Likewise when we turn back under the Thelwall Viaduct on the Trans-Pennine Trail which runs along the course of the old railway, I am left floundering and blaming Dr Beeching (wrongly as it turns out) for the railway's closure. Things came to a head one day when, on one of these rambles, a friend shouted "My God's what's that ?" It was a ship appearing to plough its way across the fields on the horizon. "Oh that " I said "That's just the Ship Canal" casually writing off the biggest civil engineering project this country had ever seen as if it were an afternoon's DIY.

The penny finally dropped as I realised that here in Lymm we are sitting on a condensed history of the whole of the Transport Revolution from the country's first purpose built canal to the massive motorway bridges of the M6. This summer for the first time there was a chance to appreciate some if not all of this amazing transport heritage with the inaugural Lymm Historic Transport Day. As I listened to some of the visitors and exhibitors at the event enthusing over their passion, be it trains, cars, bicycles, tractors or boats it occurred to me that this would be a good time to bring some of this knowledge together and tell the story of Lymm and how it has become the place it is today directly as a result of that Transport Revolution.

I am fortunate enough to have been joined in this project by Alan Taylor. Alan has lived in Lymm all his life. Retired now, he was a press photographer who in his spare time has been steadily clicking away on his camera for well over fifty years documenting changes in the village. There is potentially a lot more to come from that collection but in this volume his pictures and his editing skills have helped to give life and meaning to the written word.

We hope you enjoy the read and remember, next time you are out with your own visitors and they ask you "Which came first? the railway or the canal ? " you will be able to look them in the eye and say with calm authority " I've got this book somewhere.."

LYMM'S TRANSPORT TIMELINE

1734	Butchersfield Canal opens on the Mersey cutting out river loop that came to Statham.
1761	First section of Bridgewater Canal completed. Worsley to Salford.
1777	Extension of Bridgewater Canal through Lymm opens. Packet Boat service starts.
1824	Warrington-Stockport Turnpike opens and , with it, Lymm Dam. New stage-coach services.
1845	Chester & Mcr District Railway through Frodsham, Great Budworth and Lymm proposal.
1849	Horse-drawn omnibus service starts operation from Lymm to railway station at Altrincham.
1853	W'ton & Stockport Railway - Lymm and Heatley & Warburton railway stations open.
1863	The Rixton & Warburton Bridge Act -permitting a toll road to be built over the Mersey.
1873-1878	Mersey & Irwell Regatta at Warburton Bridge.
1891	Ship Canal starts to operate as far as Saltport at entrance to Weaver Navigation.
1894	Manchester Ship Canal opens with new cantilever bridge in place at Warburton.
1899	Electric tramway from Warrington through Lymm to Knutsford proposed
1901	Liverpool Self-propelled Traffic Association motor-car trial passes through Lymm.
1906	First Bus service to Warrington from Lymm. (not confirmed).
1909	Mass protests by cyclists in Rostherne.
1938	Church Road widened across the dam to cater for increased traffic.
1938	Manchester "Ringway" Airport – opens for passenger traffic.
1955	Lymm Cruising Club formed.
1962	Lymm and Heatley & Warburton stations closed to passenger traffic.
1963	M6 Thelwall Viaduct opens.
1969	Lymm first car park and parking restrictions.
1971	Breach at Dunham closes the Bridgewater Canal – effective end of commercial traffic.
1972	National Waterways Rally at Lymm.
1973	Bridgewater Canal re-opens.
1974	M56 Lymm junction with M6 opens.
1985	Last freight trains run though Lymm.
1995	Second Thelwall Viaduct opens.
2001	Trans-Pennine Trail officially opened.
2012	Tour of Britain Cycle Race passes through Lymm.
2013	HS2 rail-line proposals announced with major implications for East of Lymm.
2013	June 23rd The inaugural Lymm Historic Transport Day.

The Age of Horsepower

THE ENGINE THAT DROVE THE VILLAGE

FROM THE MIDDLE AGES IT WAS THE HORSE that provided the engine to power every town and village across the countryside and it continued to be a vital aspect of local transport through the Industrial Revolution and surprisingly far into the twentieth century. In Lymm, horses drew the ploughs and later towed the barges that gave the village its living. They pulled the carts at special events such as the annual May Queen parade. They carried goods to market and were the only means for people to travel at anything above walking pace.

The role of the horse was so central to life in Lymm that it was apparently even used to describe a person with strong local roots. In 1900 local photographer and author Pel Ardern explains in his book "Lymm".

"Up to about 1881 a rushcart paraded the streets each Rushbearing, drawn by grey horses, from which fact is derived the name still applied to natives of Lymm, viz "A Lymm Grey" generally denoting that the person so called belongs to a good old Lymm family.

Incidentally there is also a less noble explanation for the origin of the term "Lymm Grey" which links it to cock-fighting. Either Mr Ardern knew better or he chose to protect local sensitivities.

ABOVE: Taking a break at the Cross. In the background on the left is the old fire station and to the right the lodge cottage for Lymm Hall.

LEFT: A towing horse (see the boat behind) takes a working lunch having just passed under the village bridge.

Looking up from the lower dam. On the right are some of the many three-storey fustian cutters' cottages that were built all over the village in the late nineteenth century. The carts would have been stopped to enable a photograph to be taken .

These days the normal test for a "Lymm Grey" is some-one whose grandparents all hail from Lymm. The author goes on to talk about "Statham Blacks" based on the same logic, though this expression seems to have all but died out.

The horse provided the trade routes in and out of the village, firstly pulling carts and later barges. Lymm itself was probably too small to be a market centre but the towns of Warrington and even Manchester were both within reach. The latter was less than five hours away by horse and cart and with the Industrial Revolution which brought rapid population growth the new conurbation had an insatiable need for cheap vegetables like the potatoes produced in Lymm. Local farmer Mr Lancaster even found a market for hay as far afield as Oldham and would have two lorries, drawn by a pair of horses each, out making a delivery while two more loaded up .

Without the horse there would have been no canal through Lymm. The whole economic case for the Bridgewater Canal was based on the fact that a horse pulling a barge could carry ten times the weight of a pack horse, halving the price of coal almost overnight. It was horses bringing rough twill cloth from Manchester that opened up the whole fustian cutting trade that was central to the Lymm economy, especially in the second half of the nineteenth century.

The team proudly show off the new fire tender (inscribed with the word Lymm on the side) outside the council offices at the top of Whitbarrow Road .

The offices were built to house the new Lymm Urban District Council at the end of the nineteenth century.

The village was also a stop along several coach routes including Manchester to Liverpool and Chester, though before the opening of the turnpike road near the village centre in 1824 these must have been very uncomfortable and unreliable journeys. So it is not surprising that, when the Bridgewater Canal opened through Lymm in 1777, a regular packet boat service to Manchester was introduced almost immediately. These fly-boats would be pulled by more than one horse and rider and claimed to be able to maintain a speed of 6mph without so much as a jolt or bump.

The purchase of a horse a hundred years ago , just like today, was a significant outlay as well as having daily running costs. Parish council records for 1912 record the purchase of two bay geldings for £65 and £58 – the equivalent to several thousands of pounds in today's money. A good horse would be assigned more than one task. When the fire bell rang at the new Fire Station on Brookfield Road, that was the signal not just for the volunteer firemen to come running but for the horse to be unhitched from Billy Hinton's coal cart and led up to pull the fire tender.

SAFE. CHEAP, AND FAST
TRAVELLING,
FROM THE WHITE LION HOTEL
UNIVERSAL COACH OFFICE,
By the following fast four-inside Coaches :
MANCHESTER EMERALD, every morning at 11 o'clock,
by way of Frodsham, Preston Brook, Warrington, Altrincham,
and Lymm to the Swan Inn, Market-street, in four hours
and a half.

This advertisement appeared in 1828

Lymm Urban District Council was created in 1894 as part of a major development in local government. One of their first tasks would have been to buy horses for the many tasks for which the council was now responsible.

John Shufflebottom on the right is leading the LUDC cart which local wags referred to as standing for "Lymm Useless Donkey Cart."

The photograph was taken on street cleaning day on Church Road just opposite the end of Elm Tree Road. The words "Other Parties" top left are on the front of Lymm's Temperance Hotel . The whole sign is visible on the chapter heading page about cycling.

A thriving business in the ideal location—just to the side of the village's Plough Hotel and within 100 yards of the railway station that would provide much of the firm's business. The grander cabs would be ideal for weddings .. and funerals too.

F. Wilson,

CAB PROPRIETOR,

Plough Hotel Livery and Bait Stables,

.... LYMM.

CARRIAGES and FLYS on Hire

· AT MODERATE PRICES·

The coming of the railway in 1853 did replace many longer horse-driven journeys, but the horse was still essential in the late Victorian and Edwardian eras with a key role as the cab service for local businessmen returning by train from Altrincham and Manchester to their new suburban homes. Arthur "Cabby" Wilson ran his business from Booth's Hill Road but he also had a rank at The Plough Hotel (now The Lymm) for visitors and for commuters who found the walk too long. A trip to the end of Oughtrington Lane would cost 1s 7d – or 8p - which would have felt more like £7 or £8 based on today's values. Not surprising then that many chose to walk.

Even the introduction of the motor-car did not lead immediately to the disappearance of the horse as a mode of transport. In fact the very first car in Lymm in 1900 was often towed home by a horse after an adventurous excursion. And the two new bay geldings that arrived in 1912 were equipped by local tradesmen: Mr Druce the saddler and harness maker of Bridgewater Street (today the site of Saddlers bar) and Mr Clarke the wheelwright and blacksmith of Heatley, who provided two carts. A horse and cart was still the favoured mode of transport for many local tradesmen too, well into the 1920s. Motor transport was still considered to be unreliable, especially in cold weather.

Fred Ingham (left) ran a butcher's shop in Heatley. The shop was handily placed opposite The Green Dragon and there was a handbell just inside the shop that could be heard in the pub just in case Fred was off the premises .

After a busy day delivering to the surrounding areas like High Legh Fred could safely take a well earned nap and rely on the horse to get them both home, anticipating the "self-drive" car by a hundred years!

The picture is taken outside The Spread Eagle Hotel —notice the advertisement for petrol. Change is coming. On the right is Charles Heaven who ran the Railway Hotel.

At weekends visitors would pour in to the village by wagonette or horse-drawn double decker buses from Warrington and Manchester. The village was then, and still is, a breath of fresh air for those from the nearby industrial towns. Some arrived determined to have a good time. Mr Burrows of Lymm recalled in the late 1960s how as a boy in the early years of the twentieth century wagons would arrive drawn by three horses abreast: usually packed with women. They would tour the village before ending up at the Church Inn to quench their thirst and let off steam.

It sounds from this news report as if these visitors were lucky to get home at all. Horses were often expected to pull enormous loads and many paid the ultimate price.

A more sedate trip at the turn of the century, an Oughtrington Sunday School outing to Frodsham Hill, had a less happy outcome. A double decker bus towed by horses had been hired to take a party of children to Frodsham Hill but one of the horses fell ill on the journey and the passengers had to get out and push on the hills. When they eventually made it back to Oughtrington the poor horse dropped dead.

While this was certainly not the last horse-drawn commercial journey in Lymm, it does rather feel as if the sun was beginning to set on an era.

The Age of Horsepower was represented at Lymm Historic Transport Day by Sheldon's Dairy of Knutsford.

The first motor bus services reportedly started around 1906, though the trams from Warrington never reached nearer to Lymm than Latchford. By the beginning of the Great War in 1914, there seemed to be more horses and carts in the FOR SALE column than in the WANTED. Business on the Ship Canal was building up and remained steady on the Bridgewater; the railway was well established for commuters. The bicycle had become a massively popular means of getting about and there was a steady growth in the number of motor cars. Each of these new forms of transport presented problems to local people as well as opportunities, but one thing was certain. There would be no going back.

RIGHT: This beautiful image, taken from a lantern slide, is on Mill Lane.at Heatley. The load will almost certainly have been going to or from Thornley's Mill in Warburton which was demolished at the end of the 1990s to make way for Old Mill Close.

The Most Extraordinary Thing

THE DUKE OF BRIDGEWATER'S CANAL

THE FUTURE OF LYMM, ITS CHAR-
ACTER AND DEVELOPMENT, was
effectively laid out as the result of one English nobleman's visit to France in the 1750s.

When the Duke of Bridgewater saw the Canal du Midi,
he began to understand what could be achieved
through canal engineering and how it could solve his
problem of how to transport coal to Manchester at an
economic price. He engaged James Brindley to build
the first section of the Duke of Bridgewater's Canal
and the first stage from Worsley to Salford was duly
completed in 1761. Sceptics were quickly silenced. A
horse that had previously pulled three tons of coal by
cart could now haul ten times that amount. The price
of coal fell by fifty per cent in just a year.

One of Brindley's most imaginative decisions was to
build an aqueduct over the River Mersey at Barton. It
led one contemporary commentator to observe: " I see
ships sailing over ships ... the most extraordinary
thing in the kingdom .. if not Europe". .

One of the stars of the show at Transport Day. Originally built as a horse drawn tank-boat, Gifford now resides at the National Waterways Museum, Ellesmere Port. It was a three day trip to tow her to Lymm.

This cottage lost a corner to the canal .. It may have been as part of the later widening rather than during original building.

Brindley had a reputation for taking to his bed to solve knotty engineering problems. He was later to use the same approach to come up with a design for smaller aqueducts like the one over Whitbarrow Road.

The second phase of the canal was initiated almost immediately and would bring the canal through Sale, Altrincham and Lymm to Runcorn and from there connect to the River Mersey via ten locks. The rest of the canal was entirely lock free, speeding up movement and so reducing transportation costs. This meant building major embankments in places but also choosing the optimum line following, where possible, the contours of the land. Certain restrictions were placed on the route in the enabling Act of Parliament by those with a powerful enough voice. One clause ensured that *"no part of the intended canal or towing paths, should be nearer than fifty yards to the dwelling of the Revd Domville Halstead in Lymm aforesaid (Lymm Hall) ."*

The street name survived—the square didn't .

The villagers themselves appear to have had little or no say in the matter. As a result the canal came straight through the village square. This meant taking a slice off the corner of one cottage and building a wall in front of a row of others to accommodate a bridge. There was no public enquiry in 1766. It was not until 1777, after a protracted legal wrangle with the owner of Norton Priory that the canal was finally completed and opened for its entire length.

These cottages .. built in 1733 would have had a fine view of the square ... for the first forty years of their life.

19

To the Duke, Lymm was probably just a stop along the way between Manchester and the Mersey that could be relied on as a good spot for the stabling of horses and for refreshment and supplies for those on

Unloading coal—what the canal was originally built for— near what is now the Youth & Community Centre.

the boats. But soon the canal was to have a far greater impact on the village and its development. With transportation being advertised for as a little as 5/- a ton, it provided an attractive alternative to carting for farmers trying to get perishable goods like potatoes to market. Wharves were established along the canal. The larger ones, employing permanent staff, were known as stations. There was one in the centre of Lymm and another, still standing, at Burford Lane.

Lymm escaped most of the physical ravages of the Industrial Revolution experienced by many nearby towns like Salford and Leigh, but the huge growth in manufacturing meant that factory owners were constantly looking for new sites to build where they could also find a workforce. Early in the nineteenth century the owners of the cotton twill cloth businesses in the Manchester area found both in Lymm. Rough twill cloth could be transported cheaply along the canal and worked by a skilled cutting process into a basic corduroy velvet called fustian for labourers' clothing. Rows of three storey cottages were built with one long continuous room across the top in which to lay out the cloth for cutting on huge tables. Some of them still stand today like the ones on Church Road near the junction of Elm Tree Road. The uncut cloth would be brought from Manchester and dropped off either at a station or simply left on the side of the canal from where it could be carted to the cutters' workrooms.

Within months of the extended canal opening in 1777 a regular packet-boat service from Stockton Heath to Manchester started which helped put Lymm on the map. It may even have been from one of these boats that businessmen spotted Lymm's potential for the fustian trade. The early service was no express though. The eighteen mile journey was advertised as taking five hours including a couple of ten minute stop at Lymm and Altrincham where the horses could be changed.

There were clearly recognised class distinctions too, just as the railways would have nearly a hundred years later, advertising first class passage in the grand cabin for 2s 6d with "inferior " accommodation at just 1s 6d. One traveller, George Head (almost certainly in first class) wrote in 1835:

"This mode of travelling to an easy going individual, provided it be not repeated too often, is far from disagreeable; - without troubling himself with the world's concerns, he sits basking in sunshine and glides tranquilly onwards through a continuous panorama of cows, cottages and green fields."

The view could even be admired from the benches on the boat's flat roof. The writer was rudely awakened from his idyll as he got nearer to Manchester where *"the water is black as the Styx and pestiferous from the gas and refuse of the manufacturers with which it is impregnated."*

George Head may have been fortunate enough to have been travelling on the Duchess Countess which was built earlier in the century. If so, then as a first class passenger, he would have enjoyed a heated, carpeted cabin and afternoon tea en route.

The fingular utility arifing to the public, from the certain and expeditious conveyance along his Grace the Duke of Bridgewater's canal from London or Stockton Bridge, near Warrington, to and from Manchefter, by his paffage boats, induces us to give our readers the following authentic account of their fetting out and coming in.

New Paffage Boat fets out from Stockton Bridge, Monday, Wednefd. Friday, } At one o'clock in the afternoon.
Arrives at Caftle Quay Manchefter, at 6 o'clock the fame evening.
Sets out from Manchefter, Tuefday, and Thurfday, } At 8 o'clock each morning;
Saturday, at three o'clock in the afternoon; arrives at Stockton Bridge in five hours after.
Fare in the grand cabin 2s. 6d. Inferior cabin 1s. 6d. each paffenger.

Old Paffage Boat fets out from Stockton Bridge, Sunday, at 1 o'clock in the afternoon,
Tuefday, and Thurfday, } at 8 o'clock in the morning,
Saturday, at 5 o'clock in the morning; arrives at Manchefter in five hours after.
Sets out from Caftle Quay, Manchefter,
Monday, Wednefd. Friday, } at 8 o'clock in the morning.
Saturday, at 4 o'clock in the afternoon; arrives at Stockton Bridge in 5 hours after.
Fare 1s. each paffenger.

N. B. Children on the lap pay nothing.

The barges from Stockton Quay arrive at Altringham in three hours, ftop there and at Lymm ten minutes each, for the convenience of paffengers; the diftance from Caftle Quay at Manchefter to Altringham is 8 miles, from Altringham to Lymm 6 miles, from Lymm to Stockton Bridge or Quay 6 miles, and from thence to Warrington 1 mile. A Flat fails every day from Liverpool with goods for Manchefter, &c. and one fails alfo from Caftle Quay, Manchefter, every Tuefday, Thurfday, and Saturday at 4 o'clock each day, with goods for Warrington, Chefter, Liverpool, &c.

Freight and tonnage from Stockton Quay to Manchefter 5s. per ton.

The original advertisement for the new packet boat service in 1777.

Lymm Wharf which fell prey to the developers at the end of the 1990s. Sadly it seemed at the time that as fast as Lymm was creating its own heritage trail it was knocking down its heritage.

The packet-boats seem to have earned a reputation for achieving high speeds of six or seven miles an hour and at one time claimed to be able to complete the journey from Stockton Heath to Manchester in three hours. But this was not George Head's experience. Even though the company had by now been operating for sixty years he described the boat as being pulled by a couple of "clumsy cart-horses" that were ridden by two twelve year-old boys who alternately rode, then jumped off and ran alongside showing little evidence of any skills in horsemanship. As a result the advertised five-hour journey ended up as six. The boat then turned round almost immediately and set off on the return trip with fresh horses but the same boys.

In 1835 the packet-boat made a leisurely alternative to the jolting and bumping of the stagecoach which was the only other option. But even then the first steam train services were running between Liverpool and Manchester on Stephenson's Rocket, and by 1873 there would be three lines between the two cities including one through Lymm. Nevertheless the Duchess Countess hung on as a passenger service until 1868 though by this time it was carrying anything and everything that would pay including parcels, poultry and even cattle. It was a frequent and welcome visitor to Lymm and the image of it sailing through the village at Lymm Bridge has been widely reproduced. The boat continued to operate in occasional light service until around 1916. It was eventually broken up in the 1950s though the plans survive and the Duchess Countess Trust has aspirations to build a replica.

The Duchess Countess coming under the village bridge in the early years of the twentieth century.—no longer horse-drawn.

The Duke was always keen to maximise the return on his investment and to move as much cargo as he could as efficiently as possible. So, while the pulling power of the horse had provided the initial justification for building the canal, the Duke experimented with steam from as early as 1799. However one of the challenges was to increase speed without the wake from the boats damaging the banks. For whatever reason, plans were put to one side and the Duke died in 1803 without seeing steam in service.

In spite of all the advances in engineering the horse remained the sole source of power on the canal for its first hundred years though from time to time there were experiments which seemed promising but then came to nothing.

A report from 1841 tells of a steam trial through Lymm. The trip to Preston Brook from Manchester was made at an average speed of just over four mph including all stoppages (which was considered to be

ANOTHER CANAL STEAMER FITTED WITH MR. P. TAYLOR'S REVOLVING SCREW SCULLERS.

On Thursday, the 6th instant, we understand this new steamer made her first appearance upon the Bridgewater canal, taking in tow and tugging a timber float from Manchester to Preston Brook, distant about 25 miles, which she performed, including all stoppages and interruptions from other boats, in about six hours. She returned the same day to Manchester with three fly boats belonging to the Bridgewater trust, viz, the *Harriet*, the *Frank*, and the *Granville*, all deeply laden, and containing 60 tons of merchandise. The first and second six miles were each respectively performed in one hour and twenty-three minutes. She was accompanied for a considerable distance by several gentlemen connected with the Bridgewater Trust, who kindly afforded every assistance in conducting both that and the subsequent trials. At Lymm she was inspected by Trafford Trafford, Esq., who got on board, to whom the machinery was shewn and explained. He expressed himself much pleased with the contrivance and arrangement of the machinery, and there seemed to be but one opinion as to the successful performance. The little agitation produced by the propellers is confined to the middle of the canal, and consequently does not wash the banks so as at all to injure them.

The original news report with the exciting story of new technology on the Bridgewater canal in 1841.

Another of Lymm's lost hostelries near today's Youth and Community Centre. It was popular with boatmen for obvious reasons. There is no permanent fence in front as this was an area for loading and unloading.

impressive) and on the return journey the steam powered boat towed three fly boats, laden with 60 tons of merchandise. It must have made an awe inspiring sight coming round the bend from Statham into the village. It was met in Lymm by an official party that included the splendidly named Trafford Trafford, the squire of Oughtrington Hall, who was given a tour of the craft and its machinery. All were agreed that it had been a very successful performance causing little or no damage to the banks.

Even this successful experiment did not result in working tugs, and further developments had to wait until the trustees sold their canal to railway interests in 1872. The new Bridgewater Navigation Company had the young Edward Leader Williams as its first general manager and engineer , who came from the steam-conscious Weaver. He very quickly commissioned and introduced a fleet of steam tugs, many of them named after places on the Bridgewater Canal. These included the *Burford* and the *Lymm*. The first of these tugs went into operation in 1875, the same year that Williams moved to Dunham Massey from where he could view his acquisitions on a daily basis. Even greater projects still lay before him. Within a few years he would be commissioned as the lead architect for the Manchester Ship Canal.

The *Lymm* was a "live-in" tug with a crew of three, skipper, engineer and lad who lived in a tiny aft cabin with three box beds, a table cupboard and stove. This was no quaint rose and castle decorated craft. It was painted black with crimson side panels and distinctive funnels with two narrow white bands. The funnel was also hinged so that it could be quickly lowered to pass under the bridges that were built before steam power had even been envisaged. The *Lymm* had a long working life on the Bridgewater and probably the Ship Canal too until 1947 when she was sold to a Liverpool based company as a general purpose tug. Like so many of the early steam craft she was broken up in the 1960s.

The cottage at the village bridge is regularly seen on calendars and in magazine articles but even in the fifties this was no "chocolate-box" location.

Peter (Matthew) Corbett and his wife Sallie were taking a break from touring the Sooty Show in the early nineties . They admired the village as they came through on a narrow boat and made a mental note to return. When they did come back they discovered that the cottage was for sale. "It seemed like fate" explained Peter and they have been here ever since. Peter and Salllie are keen boaters and proud owners of "Midnight".

Peter was patron of the first Historic Transport Day in 2013.

Canal traffic started to decline after the end of the First World War. When all the working boats were handed back to their private owners after a period of war service, many companies simply couldn't afford to make up the backlog of maintenance. In spite of this, working boats continued to be a regular sight in Lymm up to the 1950s, though volumes went into steady decline in the face of increased competition from road and rail freight. By the end of the decade though there would be a radical shift in canal usage.

In 1951 the rules restricting pleasure boats on the Bridgewater were finally relaxed and cabin cruisers started to appear and eventually to outnumber the commercial traffic. These were pioneer days. Many people saw the cut as something associated with the grimy world of industry and could not understand where the "pleasure" in pleasure boating lay. Derek Hook recalled that when he came to view a house on Maltmans Road in the 1960s, the estate agent did his best to hide the canal at the bottom of the garden. He obviously felt this would damage his prospects of making a sale.

Lymm's role as a centre for canal cruising started one afternoon in 1953 when Fred Staithes was out for a spin in his car looking for a new country cottage for himself and his wife.

Work gets underway at the Cruising Club's new site . This was June 1959. .In the background is Dairy Farm which would soon make way for the Dairy Farm Estate . To the left is Oder. This was the last wooden barge owned by the Manchester Ship Canal Company who presented it to the club for conversion into a floating club house.

He stopped at the Old No 3 pub in Little Bollington where he spotted the canal boat called *Thora* moored on the bank adjacent to the inn.

It was love at first sight. Within an hour Fred had found the owner and made the purchase. He then just had to explain to his wife that there was now another woman in his life.

Within weeks Fred and his wife had teamed up with another enthusiastic local boat-owner, Eric Hurd, and together they went on to establish the Lymm Cruising Club in 1955. Originally based at Agden, the club's growth coincided with the final stages of the downturn in commercial traffic. As a result in 1959 the club were offered the National Coal Board's old wharf near the centre of Lymm for the princely sum of £500, though in those days that still involved serious fundraising.

Lymm Cruising Club—2013

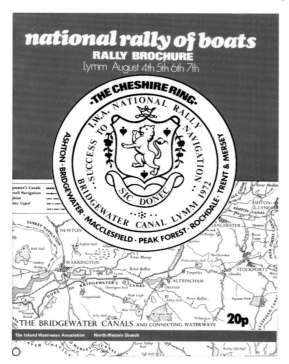

Huge crowds attended the National Rally of 1972.

A clubhouse was established in 1962 which was then extended in 1971. A plaque was made for the opening ceremony - though the bottom half was later removed when the guest of honour who had been due to unveil it failed to show up! The enlarged clubhouse was completed just in time for what was to be the Cruising Club's finest hour: the National Boat Rally of 1972.

Canals pose very different maintenance problems to roads and railways. The wear and tear on the banks is less visible but when they fail the consequences can be catastrophic. The Bridgewater Canal has always been at greater risk in this regard, as large sections of it are built on artificial embankments to avoid the need for locks. In 1829 the Manchester Advertiser reported a breach at "Bolling Bank" near Lymm when the canal burst its banks on both sides:

"In consequence the district around has been drenched with water and great damage sustained by the occupiers of the land."
Incredibly the paper reported that, while many boats had been left high and dry and that "stops" had not been closed in good time, it was nevertheless expected that the canal would re-open in eight to ten days.

Another breach—near the old coal wharf—now the site of Lymm Cruising Club, and a chance for a adventure.

Over the years there have been many such breaches. In 1931 there was a break in the canal bank where the coal yard used to be situated near to the Whitbarrow Aqueduct. The spot can still be recognised by the concrete buttress which was erected to reinforce the canal wall .

A breach near to what was then the Boathouse pub at Agden Bridge. Frantic work is going on to create a temporary dam .

The breach at Dunham in 1971 that could have signalled the end for the Bridgewater Canal. To appreciate the scale of the disaster look at the three people in the centre of the image. Remember the average depth of the canal when in proper order was around five feet.

But the burst which was to have the most far-reaching impact on the canal was the Dunham breach of 1971. The initial leak occurred at a point near the Bollin Aqueduct at Dunham some thirty feet above the river level. This quickly turned into a torrent as water gushed into the river below, washing out a gorge in the embankment ninety feet wide.

Rumours circulated that it was the end for the Bridge-water. Commercial traffic had virtually ceased anyway. In response to this situation the Inland Waterways Association announced that it would hold its National Rally at Lymm in 1972 to draw attention to the crisis. Over 500 boats attended, including a Dunkirk veteran, *The Albatross*. It is a measure of the state of the job market in 1972 that a Royal Navy recruiting team brought their canal touring exhibition; surely the only time that both a guided missile destroyer and a Polaris submarine have been spotted on the Bridgewater, even if they were slightly reduced in scale.

By the time the rally took place work had begun on repairing the breach, overseen by a newly formed trust, and the canal re-opened in 1973. But by then it was too late to revitalise commercial traffic and the last of the true working boats passed through Lymm the following year. Their place was taken by pleasure boats of all shapes and types and Lymm took on a new life as a boating destination. Today the towpath is popular with walkers, cyclists and anglers, while having "the cut" at the bottom of your garden is a pleasure to be prized rather than an eyesore to be hidden away.

Forty years after its re-opening, the canal formed the centre-piece of Lymm's first **Historic Transport Day** in June 2013, attracting historic working boats from all over the North West and the Midlands along with many pleasure boats who joined in celebrating Lymm's unique transport heritage. The afternoon culminated in a sail past of historic working boats.

Thames Conservancy Tug Kennet coming through Lymm Bridge. The Kennet now resides on the Weaver. Getting to Lymm involved removing the funnel and superstructure to allow her to negotiate the tunnels at Preston Brook.

Mimi & Richard Alderman won the prize for the longest journey to get to Historic Transport Day. They set off from Broxbourne on the River Lea on April 12 on a trip that included such cultural highlights as The Olympic Park, The Regents Canal and Birmingham's Gas St. Basin. After Lymm which they described as "the friendliest place we've been" they continued north and finally got home in October—667 locks and 885 miles later.

BELOW—THE Lorenz family entertaining friends on their beautiful Humber Keel boat—"Pauline" built in 1869.

A boater examining that most vital and mystifying piece of essential canal journey equipment—his mobile phone.

During Lymm Festival over 200 children from local primary schools had the opportunity to take part in half day canal heritage education session where they learnt about canal linked skills—everything from traditional rag-rug making to bridge building.

There was also an opportunity to visit the tiny cabins on Gifford and Saturn where a family of four would all have lived together.

The education was provided by a team from the National Waterways Museum at Ellesmere Port and the Saturn Fly-boat Project .

In the early 1900s Saturn was a regular visitor to Lymm—She is the last of the Shropshire Union fly-boats that made express deliveries of cheese to Manchester.

Pictured below, children from Statham School had the extra treat of a free canal trip from Bars bank Lane to the village thanks to the historic trip boat Castlefield which ran several cruises over the weekend to Dunham and Walton.

Crowds packed the towpath to watch the sail past of historic working boats—over twenty of them in all. There were more boats at the National Rally in 1972 - but as a gathering and display of Historic Working Boats this was probably unsurpassed on the Bridgewater Canal in living memory .

LEFT : Taking a well-earned rest on the "butty" Ilford.

TOP: The Humber Keel Pauline

CENTRE: One of the oldest boats in the show the Elizabeth originally built late 19th century.

BOTTOM: Ilford in the village centre.

The party's over. The Severn heads out towards Statham and to the winding hole for a tricky turning operation before making its way home. Severn is officially described as a short boat. I think I would call it a wide boat! She was built in 1936 for Canal Transport Services of Liverpool and worked for many years on the Leeds & Liverpool Canal.

THE FUSTIAN CUTTERS OF LYMM

In 1862 agriculture was still the main occupation of Lymm but out of a population of less than 4,000 over 700 were now employed in fustian cutting. The availability of a workforce coupled with the ability to transport heavy merchandise simply and cheaply from Manchester made Lymm an attractive proposition for

girls in Lymm, which should have had a roll of over 200, had just 70 students. The schoolmistress at the time explained *"most are taken away and set to cutting before they are nine years old and they never return -never in prosperous times at least".*

"most are taken away and set to cutting before they are nine"

the fustian masters. Like many trades that developed out of the industrial revolution fustian cutting relied heavily on child labour. In the 18thcentury, before that revolution, only around a third of ten year old working class boys in England were in the labour force. By the middle of the 19th century this figure had almost doubled. The local national school for

The pay was low too – about half that of an agricultural labourer. Taking children so young out of a stable home environment denied them their childhood or any meaningful education, either academic or social. Many of the fustian cutters, of all ages, developed a reputation as being hard-drinking and foul-mouthed with low morals. But these were an exploited

workforce and certainly not all of them fitted this stereotype. They suffered ill-health including bronchial infections and defects of the figure from standing in one unnatural position. The work was inanely repetitive yet required careful co-ordination of hand and eye. There was little or no prospect of advancement. Work was strictly on a piecework basis so a mistake was money lost. One young man, James Hart, was brought before the magistrate in 1884. The Manchester papers reported that he had been charged with..

"wilfully transmitting a piece of fustian which had been exposed to infection from scarlet fever without previously disinfecting it . The fustian was sent to Manchester along with 20 other pieces against the orders of the inspector"

A row of 19th century cottages built with an open plan top storey for laying out the cotton twill cloth.

This one features an unusual external brick staircase giving access to the workshops.

The magistrate, Mr Ridgeway was very concerned about the seriousness of the offence but the case was not pressed *"out of pity for the defendant's position."*

The implication was that there was surely scarlet fever in the boy's home and his pay was probably vital to keep the rest of the household fed.

"The cutting shop owner offered her mother a sovereign to allow the young girl to become apprenticed"

Families who had worked in the trade would do all they could to keep their own children out of it. Mrs Guest recalled in the late sixties how at the turn of the 20th century her mother had been determined that her daughter should not follow her into the trade. Mr Cowper, a well-known cutting shop owner in the village, offered her mother a sovereign to allow the young girl to become apprenticed to the trade. But he did not succeed. Instead she began an apprenticeship in dressmaking with a Miss Forrest who ran her business from near Lymm Station catering for the new middle-class clientele . The surroundings were certainly better but the work was unpaid for the first two years !

Itinerant salesmen were a regular feature at the Ship Canal and other large construction sites. They sold food and drink, workman's tools and, as here, clothing. The rough garments they were selling to the navvies were almost certainly fustian. The cloth became so associated with the working man that some radical elements of the working class chose to wear fustian as a symbol of their class allegiance.

The fustian trade lasted into the 20th century before finally closing down with the rapid decline of the Lancashire cotton trade. It had meant a harsh working life for thousands that was worlds away from the image of the picturesque rural escape portrayed for visitors to the village.

The cutter's knife

LIFE AT A CANAL WAREHOUSE

Life at Burford Lane Warehouse near Lymm between the wars was still a hive of activity. The telegraph line that linked the warehouse, Lymm and the canal offices was busy all day with boat bookings and orders. The man in charge was Oswald Hetherington Warham. He took up the post in 1926 at the age of 33, by which time he had already spent almost twenty years working on the canal. One of the regular deliveries was rags to be taken to Partington Paper works. They would be hoisted into the warehouse which was still lit by gas. At night this cast an eerie shadow as rats scurried across the floor. Other regular cargoes included cotton twill cloth for the fustian cutting trade and coal.

Oswald's daughter Vera (pictured here with boatman Bob Cliffe) recalled the sound of the horses hooves over the setts in the courtyard near the stables as they pawed the ground waiting patiently for the wagon to be loaded for the trip to Partington. Later the finished rolls of paper would be loaded onto the boats for the next stage of their journey back to Manchester.

The agent's life was always hectic: paying the wages of the banksmen, collecting rents from local farmers who leased land from the Bridgewater Canal Company and taking money for the transportation of local produce such as potatoes.

"At night the gas lights cast an eerie shadow as the rats scurried across the warehouse floor"

When Oswald finally retired in 1954 after over 47 years service the Manchester Canal Company (who also owned the Bridgewater) presented him with a silver lighter, a clock, 250 cigarettes and a box of chocolates for his wife.

Today the crumbling warehouse is one of the very few reminders still standing of the Bridgewater Canal's golden age and it was given grade II listed status in 1990 thanks to the efforts of Oughtrington's Community Association.

THE REMARKABLE AFFAIR OF
"THE LYMM MYSTERY"

The Duke of Bridgewater's Canal has claimed more than its share of victims in its 250 year history. Many men died in its construction and there have been countless drownings, mostly accidental, but some in more suspicious circumstances. However, there can have been few incidents more dramatic and inexplicable than what became known in the press as "The Lymm Mystery".

It was a cold winter's day early in January 1875. One of the newly delivered steam tugs which had just begun work on the Bridgewater was making its way through the village. Suddenly to the rear the boatman saw, momentarily, a body rise to the surface and then disappear.

Quickly he moored up and ran back to the spot but could see nothing. The police were called and the canal was dragged. Eventually the body of a young woman was recovered. She was badly cut and scarred with one prominent long clean cut below one ear. She was naked apart from her boots and stockings and one kid glove. The corpse was carried to The Plough Hotel (now the Lymm) where it was laid out for a post mortem and, it was assumed, for identification.

It was concluded that the body had not been long in the water and an appeal went out for news of anyone matching the girl's description who might have gone missing. But the young woman's identity remained a mystery and, given her state of undress, foul play was strongly sus-pected. However it was difficult to decide whether some of the injuries could have been caused by the body making contact with the screw propellers of boats. When no-one came forward after two weeks, the authorities reluctantly decided that a funeral should be arranged for her in Lymm at St Mary's Church. A large crowd of

"A woman entered the churchyard and demanded to see the corpse"

local people gathered for the ceremony as the story had gripped the village. What happened next is probably best described by the news report at the time:

"Just as the funeral bell tolled a woman entered the churchyard. She demanded to see the corpse and in response to her earnest entreaties the lid was taken off

the coffin when she identified the deceased as her daughter ... a sad scene then took place and when all doubt was removed the interment of Mary Rigby aged 20 of Liverpool proceeded."

Within days a man was arrested: Watson Whiteley, a chimney sweep of Tuebrook, Liverpool. All seemed set for a swift conclusion to the affair. Mary, who was in service in Liverpool, had been having an affair with a young man who was a sweep, and another woman, Catherine Lawless testified how she delivered Mary's notes to the sweep's house. She identified Whiteley in court as that man.

But by June not only had Whiteley been cleared of the charges, but he in turn prosecuted the police for wrongful arrest and Catherine Lawless was brought to court on a charge of perjury. Whiteley had an alibi and claimed mistaken identity. He maintained that he had had a young apprentice living with him named "Joe" and that the letters were intended for him. He had returned them requesting that they stop. The case against the police was dismissed on a technicality. Young Catherine Lawless was cleared of perjury in a bitter trial that ended in a violent confrontation between Lawless and Whiteley on the steps of the court. Counter accusations flew back and fore but the mystery of why Mary was in Lymm that day, of whether she was murdered and by whom has remained to this day unsolved.

Turnpikes & Toll Bridges

FROM CART-TRACKS TO HIGHWAYS

AMONG THE FIRST THINGS THAT STRIKE TODAY'S VISITOR TO LYMM, after the famous Cross and the stocks, are the roads still laid with traditional setts on Pepper Street and Bridgewater Street. A closer look at the latter shows an arrangement of the stones that provided a smooth run for the horse-drawn carts that were pulled up the steep hill to the canalside wharf. Within the last five years the lower dam has been re-surfaced with a modern version of the sett in an effort to retain something of the character of the village.

Today these surviving setts serve as a somewhat jolting and bumpy reminder of the village's transport heritage. Yet it was only in the second half of the 19th century that they were seen as a huge advance and a welcome relief from the rutted muddy tracks that surrounded the village. One other disadvantage, apart from the jolting, was that they were noisy, and in Edwardian times it was not unknown for local people to throw down chippings or bark to deaden the noise for the benefit of those lying in their sick bed.

The setts leading up from Bridgewater Street to one of the canal wharves—looking very much the same as when they were first laid over 150 years ago.

Until well into the 19th century the maintenance of roads remained the legal responsibility of individual parishes. Men were obliged to work for six days every year to repair the highway and keep it in good order. Some would have been only too keen to see this duty fulfilled as they relied on having viable routes to transport their produce to nearby markets or to the new wharves along the Duke of Bridgewater's canal that ran through the centre of the village. However, very few villagers travelled and some may not have been particularly interested in doing their share.

In 1794 one Isaac Ridgway took responsibility for organising this task for the hamlet of Statham. He kept a full record of the days worked. Most people were conscientious with six lines drawn next to their names (one for each day) but it looks as if he may have been having trouble with the Leather family who, judging by the record, were more reluctant labourers. The list of other expenditures suggests a "make-do and mend" approach to road maintenance at that time.

With the Industrial Revolution in the late eighteenth century came the need for improved communications. All over the country turnpike roads were springing up. Authorised by Acts of Parliament and privately financed, responsibility for new road building and maintenance passed to the road's owners who were permitted to charge a toll to pay for the road's upkeep.

ABOVE: 1794, Statham is self sufficient for road maintenance.

LEFT: Over 150 years later on Warrington Road and the farmer still holds sway. Thelwall Viaduct would soon impose on this view.

Turnpike roads came late to Lymm, perhaps because of the presence of the canal, but in 1821 the Warrington and Stockport Trust was granted licence to build a highway between the two towns. The obvious route at first sight may have been through the centre of the village, perhaps even following the Mersey valley in places. But this would have presented major problems, not least because the lower route was in the flood plain of the river. Before the riverbanks were raised up, flooding was a regular hazard. A newspaper report of flooding in 1828 described the devastation:

"From Carrington to Statham and all the way to Warrington the whole valley of the river is under water; and boats are everywhere to be seen sailing over fields and amongst trees".

Local historian Joe Griffiths also points out that there was another possible route founded on an existing link between Warrington and Altrincham. One of the main roads out of the village is Pepper Street which leads to an apparent dead-end. However there is a track - known as Sutch Lane - which continues all the way to Oughtrington. Carry on from there - either along Stage Lane or the course of the canal - and you arrive at Warrington Lane. It's a road name that now seems irrelevant to its location but it indicates that this may once have been part of an older established route.

An 1850 print of the new beauty spot that was used by Pel Ardern in his early guide books to Lymm from 1900 onwards. The building below the church is the Grammar School .

fine view of the turnpike (around the turn of the 20th century?) The
ll was now lifted. The bridge is the one over the dam. The building in
e background is the Rectory on Rectory Lane. Parson's Walk led from
e Rectory to Church Road and then along a path that offered the min-
ter some privacy and some protection from the mud splashes.

time it has become a well-known beauty spot which
has drawn visitors to the village for nearly two hundred years.

The lake must have been one of the memorable sights
from the stagecoaches that soon sped past en route
between Manchester and Chester or Liverpool. The
coach companies were quick to capitalise on the new
road and by 1828 the Chester Stagecoach Company
was advertising a journey time between the two cities
of just over four hours at an average speed in excess
of ten mph. Yet the trip was more remarkable for
speed than comfort. The revolutionary road surface
developed by Macadam was still in its infancy and not
widely adopted England for at least another ten years.

This alternative might have formed the
basis of the new turnpike road, but there
was resistance to the idea of its coming
through the middle of the village. The
centre had already been radically altered
by the canal only fifty years previously
and there were concerns about congestion. Accordingly a higher route was
chosen which involved damming the
stream of the Dane just below St Mary's
church. There was already a path and a
footbridge crossing at this point but it
was a major project to create a dam, and
its installation would have been a great
talking point and attraction. The lake
which was formed by the damming was
in a sense incidental, but over a period of

This group are walking along the stretch of road shown in the picture above. Some are
wearing an emblem in their lapel but the event is not known. What is certain is that they
could confidently stride down the middle of the road without fear of meeting traffic.

When the banks of the Mersey were eventually built up and reinforced in the middle of the 19th century, much of the land around Heatley and Warburton dried out and for the first time there was the possibility of building a permanent road link from near Lymm to Lancashire. As it was a county boundary and neither Cheshire nor Lancashire were prepared to foot the bill the new Rixton and Warburton Toll Bridge could only be built following an 1866 Act of Parliament.

What was not legislated for was the possibility of the river drying up and the bridge becoming redundant, but that is exactly what happened when this stretch of the Mersey was diverted into the Ship Canal after the Lymm stretch opened in 1891. This development required the construction of an entirely separate canti-lever bridge beyond the first one.

Navvies winching up bridge sections from the river below

The "new" bridge—built to span the Ship Canal in 1890-1

The new bridge, built and paid for by the Ship Canal Company, was constructed on the same principle as the Forth Bridge. The design is light and graceful in appearance, but any increased pressure tends to knit the parts together more firmly.

For a short time, while the new bridge was being built, the link from Lymm north to Rixton was broken. It was only when this section of the canal had been filled with water that floating pontoons could be used to allow sections of the bridge to be lifted into place. One of these pontoons nearly caused a major accident when it capsized in mid-stream. It was feared that the eight men working on it would all drown, but seven of them managed to cling to a rope connected with the raft and were eventually pulled ashore. The other man was rescued from a boat. Falling in the canal always presented a double risk. As well as the possibility of drowning, there was a very real chance of picking up a serious infection—even typhoid.

Once the ship canal was in operation, the old river course could be filled in – there was no shortage of earth - and turned over to farmland. The original river bridge was replaced by an embankment and a ramp road to the ship canal crossing.

However the right to charge the toll on this stretch remains in force and that is why the folk of Lymm and surrounding areas pay twelve pence to get to Rixton. The bridge is one of eight surviving privately owned statutory tolled roads in the country. Now doesn't that make you feel special? (or about £50 a year poorer if you happen to travel that way most days).

Incidentally, spare a thought for any heavily laden cyclists you see on the bridge. They may be in the middle of a very long trip as Warburton Bridge is on one of the most commonly used routes for cycling from Lands End to John O'Groats.

Booth's Hill Road, The milepost that crossed the road.

The main turnpikes had their tolls lifted in the 1880s when legislation meant that the newly formed county councils assumed responsibility for roads. To this day though there remain visible signs of the original route: a milepost on Booth's Road, that was originally on the opposite side, and a traveller's rest stone seat that can be found, fittingly, on the roadside outside the service station on Higher Lane.

It's payback time. This cottage that used to stand on Booths Hill Road (opposite where the convenience store is now) used to act as a toll gate. With the widening of the A56 it seems to have donated its front garden to the Highways Department for a signpost.

The old traveller's rest stone from turnpike days looks a little forlorn and forgotten now in front of the Shell station. There is an inscription too somewhere under all that moss.

By the time of the appearance of the bicycle in around 1880 and the motor car in 1900, the roads locally were at least negotiable with care. But a trip to Lymm by bicycle or motor was still not for the faint hearted. This 1906 report on "How to get to Warburton from Manchester" gives a clue to the state of the roads:

"Those who do not object to rough going may branch to the right from Washway Road… through Ashton-on-Mersey. Another plan is to branch from the Chester Road at Broadheath. That way too the going is rough as is that too on a third and more roundabout one through the Dunhams …"

It was not until 1936 that important trunk roads came under the management of national government and until then there was still a very loose definition of what constituted "maintenance". As a result standards varied hugely from area to area. Local authorities were fighting for resources and one meeting of the Lymm Local Board in 1886 seems to have almost ended in fisticuffs.

SCENE AT A CHESHIRE BOARD MEETING.— At a meeting of the Lymm Local Board, held on Friday week, a sharp controversy took place between two of the members during a discussion regarding road improvements. Mr Hall, a member, asked a question as to when work was to be done in the village, respecting which money had been voted.—Mr Rogers, replying, said that Mr Hall must not be sarcastic, or he would "sit upon him." Formerly, he added, Mr Hall had been insulting, personal, and scurrilous, and he (Mr Rogers) had listened with contempt.—Mr Hall: You are so very egotistical in your remarks. I have asked a very important question.—Mr Rogers: I am not prepared to answer it.—Mr Hall repeated his question. Mr Rogers: If you would exercise a little commonsense you would do better.—Mr Buazendale thought Mr Hall justified in asking the question.—Mr Hall (to Mr Rogers): You think you will sit upon me, but you will not.—Mr Rogers: I will, but you have not sense to see when you are sat upon.—Mr Hall: I will bring you to task.—Mr Rogers: Will you?—Mr Hall: I think I am capable of taking care of myself.—Mr Rogers: Indeed you are not.—Mr Hall: Besides, I do not consider you are a member of this board. You are only just slipped in to do that which is not straightforward.—Mr Rogers: What is it? I demand an explanation.—Mr Hall was then understood to say that Mr Rogers came in an interest that had been too long dominant on the board. Mr Rogers: What interest?—Mr Hall: Is it necessary to tell you?—Mr Rogers: You may have to answer far more than you are able to answer for in another place than this.—Mr Hall: I know how far to go. You will not find me go over a certain line. I am too wide awake for that.—Mr Rogers: You are not too wide awake.— The business of the board was then proceeded with.

ABOVE: Most council meeting reports of the time are dull in the extreme . This one sounds like an altogether livelier affair that was obviously considered worth reporting verbatim.

LEFT: No wonder the Road Committee were arguing. This was the state of the road outside the Green Dragon around the turn of the century. It looks like the road maintenance team is out in force… one wheelbarrow, one policeman to control traffic and an onlooker. Inadequate roads were quickly made far worse by the churning of car tyres from 1900 onwards.

By the way that's Mr Ingham's butcher shop in the corner whom we met in "The Age of Horsepower" There are four sides of beef hanging outside !

In 1897, with the formation of the Lymm Urban District Council, there was clearly major concern over the state of the roads and the cost of repairing them. The cost of hiring a steam roller to carry out essential repairs was 30/- a day exclusive of fuel and water. The council also took responsibility for the building of a new girder bridge across the Bridgewater Canal at Brookfield Road to replace the existing wooden one. This could not proceed until Mr Dewhurst of Beechwood Hall, who owned huge tranches of land throughout Lymm, could be persuaded to release the area on either side of the proposed bridge at 2/6d per square yard - rather than the 3/9d he originally proposed and which the council considered extortionate.

Within a couple of years the first motor cars were trundling over the bridge, driving Lymm into a new century of transport innovation.

The Samson –representing the road builders of the first half of the twentieth century -at Lymm Historic Transport Day. Produced by Charles Burrel of Thetford , Norfolk. Samson worked in Cornwall for many years but has been in and around Lymm since 1986 . It is parked across three places in the pay and display car park on Pepper St. Good job it's a Sunday !

The Steam Era

RAILWAY MANIA REACHES LYMM

IT WAS A MOMENTOUS DAY FOR TRANSPORT AND FOR SOCIETY when Stephenson's Rocket pulled out of Liverpool for Manchester in October 1830. This was the first regular steam service in Britain and it was such a success that it was to unleash two waves of railway building mania. By 1845 there were already 2,000 miles of railways in England and between then and 1850 nearly another 10,000 miles of construction were sanctioned. One such scheme was the Chester and Manchester Direct Railway of 1845. This was to be a new line passing through Frodsham, Great Budworth and Lymm and then via Urmston to Manchester. Not only that but Lymm was to be a key point on the route with branches to Warrington and Altrincham. However by the late 1840s enthusiasm for new lines was fading fast as investment dividends fell and this was just one of many schemes that failed to come to fruition.

By 1849 the railway had at least reached Altrincham from Manchester and there was clearly demand for a link to Lymm as a horse-drawn bus service was set up to connect the village to the new line at Altrincham. George Arnold was advertising his new horse-drawn omnibus service in 1849.

Steaming to Lymm, 1950s—taken at Halfpenny Bridge, Statham. Camsley Lane in the background.

OMNIBUS BETWEEN LYMM AND ALTRINCHAM STATION.—The Public are respectfully informed, that an OMNIBUS has Commenced RUNNING between LYMM and ALTRINCHAM STATION; leaves Lymm Cross daily at 8 a.m. Nags Head at 8 5, Church Green at 8 15, Jolly Thrasher at 8 20 Stamford Arms Inn, Bollington, at 8 25, and Bowden at 8 40, in time for train at 9 o'clock, which arrives in Manchester at 9 25 a.m. Returns in connection with train leaving Manchester at 5 p.m.
GEORGE ARNOLD, Proprietor.

Not quite the first "replacement bus service" but a horse-drawn link-up with the new railway at Altrincham in 1849.

This innovation was revolutionary for Lymm. For the first time someone living in the village could spend the whole day in Manchester and be home by 7pm. But George Arnold's little pot of gold was short-lived for even as his coach left Lymm each morning, work was underway on the laying of the line that would connect Warrington Arpley to Broadheath via new stations at Thelwall, Lymm, Heatley & Warburton and Dunham. The Warrington and Altrincham Junction Railway was created by an Act of Parliament in 1851, and the first trains on this new Liverpool to Manchester rail link ran from October 1853. Another piece in the chaotic patchwork of private railways was complete – well almost. Delays in the delivery of iron work for the bridges over both the Mersey and the Bridgewater Canal meant that the line was initially isolated from the rest of the railway network until 1 May 1854. Even

then passenger trains terminated at Broadheath until the owners of the new line could agree with the other company's charges for passengers travelling on to Manchester via Timperley; another indication of the fragmented approach to the whole business of building a railway network.

The new line did more than anything up to that time to change the appearance and character of Lymm to how we know it today. A reasonably prosperous but essentially rural village that was based on agriculture had already started to acquire its fair share of small-scale industry, including fustian cutting, gold beating and basket making.

Lymm Station—On Christmas Day the Boumphrey family of Baycliffe would have a private saloon coach attached to the train to take them to Liverpool for a family gathering. At other times they would hitch up a horse-box to go hunting in South Cheshire and hire a locomotive to bring them home in the evening. There is no record of the cost of this extravagance.

Some of these trades relied heavily on the canal to ship raw materials in and finished products out, but nothing had fundamentally altered the peaceful "backwater" feel of the village. There were grand houses – Lymm Hall, Beechwood House, Baycliffe - occupied by what were still referred to as the gentry. However for the most part villagers lived in rows of cottages. These

A young girl proud of her new home on Higher Lane

may have later appeared "quaint" but most were very basic. Nevertheless businessmen who occasionally passed through – perhaps on the packet boat or stage coach - would have seen an attractive village with plenty of shops centred around the Cross. It made a welcome change from the smoke-filled industrial grime that was Manchester and Salford where even breathing the air near the river could cause illness.

LYMM.—TO BE SOLD by Private Contract, TWO Well-built and Convenient Freehold DWELLING-HOUSES, pleasantly situated on the Eagle Brow, in Lymm, within ten minutes' walk of the intended station on the Warrington and Altrincham Railway, and distant five miles from Warrington and fourteen from Manchester.—For particulars and to treat for the same, apply to Mr JOHN FORREST, Altrincham ; or to Mr. JOSEPH FORREST, Lymm, who will show the property.

The prospect of a station was a great selling point for Lymm in 1853

When the railway opened, some local people were quick to realise the opportunity and from the mid-Victorian period smart new houses started to spring up. Not quite gentry perhaps but the new up and coming middle classes. Some of their occupants, like the Gregson family, made their way within the village. Young James Gregson had started work as a tailor with his father near Preston but eventually moved to Lymm where he owned the mill at the Lower Dam and the bakery on Eagle Brow. After a spell living "over the shop" the family moved to one of the new houses built by the Beechwood Estate at 7 Whitbarrow Road and later on to retirement at Leckonby, number 11, in the first years of the 20th century.

The rear of Leckonby at 11 Whitbarrow Road—Coach house and gardener to the left—with, possibly, Mr & Mrs Gregson Snr

One man who saw every working day the possibilities presented by the new rail service was Mr Jones, who was one of the first station masters at Lymm. He was thrifty and gradually bought up land and invested his savings in building substantial houses in the general neighbourhood of Lymm Station. They included many of the houses on Brookfield Road (originally called Station Road). He also built 16 Whitbarrow Road, opposite the hotel, to which he retired when paralysis struck, but from where he could still watch the trains arrive and leave.

The new homes certainly contributed to the growth of the village along with the new roads and businesses. But this was no population explosion. In 1801 the village had just over 1,500 inhabitants. This doubled by 1851, but in the next fifty years the village only grew by a further 1,500. This may have been partly

Looking down Eagle Brow 100 years ago. It all looks remarkably familiar.

Important Announcement.

The LONDON & NORTH WESTERN RAILWAY COMPANY will, from October 1st, 1911, make the following improvements in the services between :—

LYMM, HEATLEY and MANCHESTER and *vice versa*,

AND BETWEEN

LYMM and WARRINGTON and *vice versa*.

A new quick service will be provided, leaving Lymm at about 6.3 p.m. and Heatley at 6.8 p.m. for Manchester, due Oxford Road at 6.36 p.m. and London Road, 6.39 p.m.

A new service will be provided, leaving Manchester (London Road) at 8.10 p.m. (Oxford Road) at 8.13 p.m., reaching Heatley, 8.35 p.m. and Lymm, 8.39 p.m.

The present 5.20 p.m. from Manchester (London Road) will leave at 5.35 p.m., and will be accelerated six minutes, reaching Lymm at 6.10 p.m.

A new service will be provided, leaving Warrington at about 5.45 p.m. for Lymm and Heatley.

The Conditions of Sale and Particulars of the Apportioned Outgoings as well as the Building Restrictions will be published in the Second Edition.

1911 and L&NWR are advertising a fast service from Manchester to Lymm in 35 minutes !! Try doing that today.

because rail services were never that frequent. As early as 1901 the council were petitioning the railway company to improve the service as they felt that the limited timetable was discouraging people from taking up residence. For a while they had some success. When the huge Beechwood Estate was sold off in 1911 it included many large homes in the vicinity of Lymm Station and the sales brochure made a special point of drawing attention to the fact that extra rail services would soon be starting. A hundred years ago it was a far easier journey to Manchester than it is today.

ABOVE: *Lymm Station 1910. A very rare picture of the early days of the railway in Lymm, - originally provided by Walter Struthers to co-author Alan Taylor. The crowds are on the westbound platform in their Sunday best. Are they heading home after a trip to Lymm for some special occasion.? May Queen perhaps ? Far left is a poster for Hilton's Boots—a well known shop on Bridgewater Street.*

RIGHT: *Excursions were running even in 1865– no luggage allowed. That would have taken up valuable human cargo space. The advertisement also proudly proclaims that third class will be a covered carriage.*

LONDON AND NORTH-WESTERN AND MANCHESTER SOUTH JUNCTION & ALTRINCHAM RAILWAY.—CHEAP TRIP TO LYMM, &c.—On Saturday, July 1, 1865, and every Saturday until further notice, a SPECIAL TRAIN will leave the Oxford-road Station, MANCHESTER, at 2 10 p.m., for DUNHAM-MASSEY, HEATLEY, LYMM, THELWALL, and LATCHFORD. Returning from Latchford at 8 30 p.m.; Thelwall, 8 35 p.m.; Lymm, 8 40 p.m ; Heatley, 8 45 p.m.; and Dunham-Massey, 8 50 p.m.

FARES THERE AND BACK :—

	1st Class.	Cov. Car.
To Dunham Massey, Heatley, or Lymm....	2s. 0d.	1s. 0d.
To Thelwall or Latchford..................	2s. 3d.	1s. 3d.

Children, full fare. No luggage allowed.—By order. Lime-street Station, Liverpool, June, 1865.

Early rail fares were higher than a stage coach on the basis that trains were quicker and more comfortable. However by the time Lymm station opened in 1853 there was a realisation that railways were for everyone albeit the masses would be huddled into very basic third class accommodation, even open to the elements at first. One hard-headed businessman summed up the case for passenger traffic like this:

"Third class passengers at fifteen to the ton yield fifteen pence per ton for haulage only as they load and discharge themselves".

However primitive the carriages may have been, they came to Lymm in their thousands. At holiday times in particular the village could be crowded with visitors. They came to the Warburton Regatta on August Bank Holiday in the 1870s, to the Rushbearing and to the May Queen Festival at Whitsun. For all these events special trains were laid on from Manchester. The council even requested that the platforms at Lymm and Heatley be lengthened as the excursion trains from Manchester often had to pull in twice to disgorge the crowds and to fill up at the end of the day.

Isn't it amazing what you find when you turn out your pockets?

Tickets marked L&NWR are 1923 or older. After that they were absorbed by London Midland and Scottish—(none of which describes Lymm of course!). Some passengers chose to travel first class even from Heatley to Lymm and for a while there were pull out ads on the tickets. They obviously knew their market - promoting whisky to the first class customers of Lymm.

We are indebted to Michael Stewart who shared part of his collection with us for this book. They really bring the railway back to life !

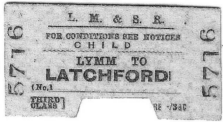

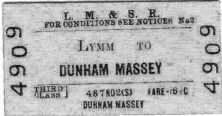

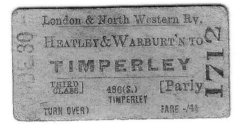

Lymm Dam was another popular destination on a weekend as was the Saracens Head at Warburton with its lake, pleasure gardens and musical entertainments. In 1913 local photographer and writer Pel Ardern despaired of the impact that the unwashed multitude was having on the local surroundings:

"How many roots of primroses and daffodils have been ruthlessly torn up by thoughtless trippers to lead a dismal drooping life in some backyard in Manchester or some other murky town!"

Is this one of Pel Ardern's "thoughtless trippers " caught in the act at Lymm Dam? By the look of her I suspect this lady has not seen too many "backyards in Manchester".

Some visitors came primarily to let off steam and the challenge for the local bobby was to get them all safely despatched back to Manchester, Warrington and Liverpool at the end of the night. There was a good meal to be had at the Saracen's Head in nearby Warburton – a chicken dinner followed by rhubarb and custard - but the beer was not really strong enough to get them sufficiently merry so revellers would move onto the Green Dragon or The Railway Hotel before taking the last train home.

FRACAS IN A RAILWAY CARRIAGE.
At Altrincham, William Frost and James Hale, brass-finishers, Salford, were charged with unlawfully wounding William Brown, of Hulme, Manchester, at Broadheath, on Saturday evening. Prisoners had been at a picnic at Lymm They got drunk and had a row in the carriage. Brown was found with serious wounds on the forehead, lying in a pool of blood.

You can't beat a nice genteel picnic .. 1896 style.

The exercise of getting them all onto the train did have some upsides as local man Mr Lancaster later recalled:

"I used to help the local policeman with the merrier customers getting the late night trains. They were bundled into the compartments and the windows were let down so that late arrivals could be thrown in at the last minute. As the worst of the drunks came up Mill Lane escorted by the constable, he would save them from further temptation by removing surplus bottles of beer from their pockets and throwing them under the hedge en route. When his charges were safely on their way the policeman would collect up the bottles and enjoy a couple each night until his stocks were replenished the following week."

I am sure this photograph does not do the prize-winning floral display justice .

For most people though the coming of the trains was a boon. Whether it was for work, shopping or social trips, Lymm was now connected with neighbouring large towns and cities. The Plough & Railway Hotel (now the Lymm Hotel) also benefited. It became an attractive base for international sports teams such as the Australian cricket eleven when they were playing at Old Trafford.

The station was now part of the fabric of village life. Jeanne Artingstall recalls how the guard would hold up the train if he saw last minute stragglers waving as they hurried down Whitbarrow Road. For many years the local council lobbied the railway company to have a footbridge between the platforms installed for safety reasons, but no-one seems to be able to recall anyone

actually ever using it. It was so much quicker just to nip across the lines. With relatively infrequent trains to service, the staff took pride in the appearance of the station and they were proud winners of the "best-kept station" competition.

The line was a favoured short cut from the Star at Statham to the station too. David Taylor remembers how his father would use it regularly until he was stopped one day in 1952 by the Transport Police and brought before the magistrate. On another occasion a couple of regulars were horrified to discover that the Star had run out of mild for their favourite pint of "mixed" so they ran down to the Plough & Railway, half a mile along the track, with a couple of glasses for the vital missing ingredient.

Lymm Station 1958 and not a soul in sight. The writing is on the wall .
Trains were few and cars were becoming plentiful.

Local resident John Gill would be on hand in the 1950s as one of the newspaper delivery boys when the 4.50pm arrived, to pick up the Manchester Evening News and Chronicle from the station. They would then sit on the red station benches and quickly sort them for immediate delivery. John recalls too that even into the 1960s when passenger services had finished one could watch the weekend seaside and football specials passing through. During the week though, you were as likely to see goods trains piled high with some of the new cars that would soon signal the death knell of so many branch lines.

In 1953 the council wrote again complaining that the last train from Manchester was now at 7.04pm. But the writing was on the wall. The last scheduled passenger train pulled out in September 1962 even before Dr Beeching had to chance to begin work on his report.

Being the slowest of three rail links between Liverpool and Manchester was just too much competition. John Gill and his friends along with many others crowded onto the last train from Oxford Road to Latchford. The beer was flowing and the atmosphere was something between a party and a wake. Just west of the village, passengers on that last train could have looked out and seen work busily progressing on the new M6 Thelwall Viaduct towering above them. It would open just nine months later.

Goods traffic, mainly carrying coal to a local power station, continued till 1985. The line was still useful but it was decided that the bridge at Latchford, which had been built to allow the Ship Canal to pass underneath, was in need of expensive major repairs and so the railway through Lymm was finally closed.

Many of those who were saddened at the loss of their local line were the same people who were now polishing their new pride and joy, their car, in the driveway on a Sunday morning.

The paraphernalia of the railway gradually disappeared. Signal boxes and station buildings were taken down. Lines were ripped up. There were some changes that people welcomed with the closure of the line. One was the removal of the level crossings that ran across many of the village's main roads like an intrusive zip. These had been a daily hold-up that had also caused many tragic accidents over the years. And with the final closure of the line John Gill and many other residents could finally sleep uninterrupted at night as the midnight mail train, which used to tear through the village at sixty mph shaking the houses on either side, had made its last delivery.

ABOVE: The signal box on Birch Brook Road or Lymm Lane as is it was called when the box was built.—It was kept open for goods traffic until 1985 and for the last ten years of its life it also supervised Mill Lane crossing by CCTV.

BELOW: One of the last trains in June 1985—heading toward Camsley Lane—Picture taken from close to same spot as the chapter opening.

A MOST SPECTACULAR NEW EVENT
THE MERSEY & IRWELL REGATTA AT WARBURTON

In 1871 The Bank Holidays Act created a new day off for the working masses "August Bank Holiday Monday". This was the first time that a holiday had been granted that was not in any way religious. It was, in the words of the bill's champion Sir Henry Lubbock, for no other reason than to "ease the lot of the most hard worked classes of the community". For many years it was affectionately known as St Lubbock's day.

Just a few years before this, Warburton Bridge had opened, spanning the Mersey and providing extensive vistas west and east. It was a popular destination for ramblers and was only a mile or so from Heatley and Warburton Station.

So it was perhaps not surprising that some enterprising soul would grasp the chance to create a new event that would use the river and also attract visitors to enjoy the new holiday. What was surprising was how quickly it grew into a public occasion of national reputation. But then just when it seemed to be destined to be an annual affair it disappeared, to be followed soon after by the river itself. This is the story of The Mersey and Irwell Regatta at Warburton.

It started in no small way on August 4th 1873. As well as the rowing races there was to be entertainment by the Bands of the 7th Dragoon Guards and the 101st Fusiliers. Advance tickets were 1s 6d or 2s 6d at the gate and there were spaces set aside for carriages and horse-drawn omnibuses. Henry Lang of The Fountain Inn in Manchester was booked to provide liquid refreshments and cold collations from two large marquees, all doubtless brought out by train from Manchester.

The first year was by all accounts a boggy affair but by the next year the event's reputation had spread and crowds more than doubled – estimated at several thousands. Crews came from as far afield as London, Newcastle, Preston and Chester, attracted, no doubt, by the generous prizes of up to 45 guineas – over £1,000 in today's money.

MERSEY AND IRWELL AMATEUR REGATTA BELOW WARBURTON BRIDGE. ON MONDAY AUGUST 4 (BANK HOLIDAY). First Race at 12 Noon.
The 9 20 a.m. Train from London-road Station will stop at Heatley Station.
A train will leave London-road at 11 o'clock, and Oxford-road at 11 5, reaching Heatley at 11 45.
A Special Train will leave London-road at 11 45.
By permission of the Officers, the BAND of the 101st FUSILIERS will be in attendance.

MERSEY AND IRWELL AMATEUR REGATTA. BELOW WARBURTON BRIDGE. ON MONDAY NEXT.
In consequence of the Regimental Sports taking place on August 4th, the Committee regret to state that the Band of the 7th Dragoon ... will not be in attendance at Warburton. Arra... in progress to replace it. ... AND IRWELL AMATEUR REGATTA, BELOW WARBURTON BRIDGE, ON MONDAY, August 4th (Bank Holiday). FIRST RACE AT TWELVE, NOON.

MERSEY AND IRWELL REGATTA, MONDAY, AUGUST 4TH, BANK HOLIDAY.
HENRY LANG, Fountain Inn, Manchester, begs to inform his Friends and the Public that he will SUPPLY REFRESHMENTS on the Committee Ground in his two large Marquees.
A COLD COLLATION will be served from twelve to four o'clock.
NOTICE.—The Fountain Inn will be Closed for that day.

The short-lived Warburton Bridge over the Mersey— site of the regatta. Sadly there are no known images of the event itself. The racecourse was from the mouth of the Bollin to the bridge.

The Manchester Times reported:

"Although most of the visitors were carried by the numerous special trains to Heatley many other parties drove down from Manchester and there were, along the riverside, a long line of carriages among them two or three drags which were turned out in excellent style."

The "drag" sometimes known as a "park drag" was the boy-racer vehicle of the time. With the coming of the railways the stage coach had quickly become redundant and many were locked away and forgotten in sheds. So by the 1870s there was

A typical four-in–hand at The Railway Hotel, Heatley —date unknown

a fashion for well to do private individuals to buy them up, decorate them attractively and drive them "four-in-hand", carrying groups of up to twelve or fifteen friends and family.

1875 and the regatta was dizzy with success. The Manchester Courier told its readers:

"Neither of the previous regattas can compare with this in the quality of the entries. Some of the best known amateur fours, pairs and scullers in the world took part in the competitions".

The 1876 regatta was another great success but was marred by the drowning of a young man who had arrived by canoe. Stepping from his boat at the point where the Bollin meets the Mersey, he capsized and was swept away by the river.

In the following two years the regatta drew crews from Downing and Trinity College Cambridge who competed alongside rowers from Eton College as well as all the national clubs. In spite of that the event seems to have taken a downward turn. Newspaper reports were more downbeat; not enough competitive races and squabbles among clubs with one refusing to compete against another.

It is likely too that by 1878 there many more competing attractions for the Bank Holiday visitor including Belle Vue in Manchester and Manley Park which held a musical fete and, as a special attraction featured the ascent of Mr Coxwell's monster balloon. There was even a rival regatta from 1874 at Pomona much to the annoyance of the Warburton organisers, though it was a less than idyllic venue by all accounts. One group of spectators were treated for diarrhoea after breathing the noxious fumes of the river. Another viewer slipped and fell in. He was dragged from the river alive but died of typhoid a couple of days later. It is no wonder that many clubs continued to be attracted to the more rural delights of Warburton.

Whatever the explanation there are no further reports of the regatta after 1878 and within another decade work had started on the Manchester Ship Canal just a hundred yards to the north of the Mersey.

Any rower returning in later years by bicycle or car on a nostalgic trip to their old haunt would have sought in vain for either bridge or river or any remnant of this once famous event. The river was filled in for farmland, the bridge became an embankment, and the landscape was now dominated by new water craft: the huge ships that made their way to Manchester under the new Warburton cantilever bridge.

OF LIFE AT HEATLEY & WARBURTON STATION

Roy Holt was born in Warburton and lived all his life in the Lymm & Heatley area, latterly on Mill Lane. Roy lost his sight during his childhood and spent time away at school. His father was for many years a manager at the Salt Works in Heatley until its closure in the 1960s. Roy loved his home village and was an active member of the local History Society He spent time recording the reminiscences of others, some of which are included in the book, before concentrating on writing down and publishing his own memories of which this story is a beautiful example.
He died in March 1998, aged 78.

As a child in the thirties I regarded Heatley station, in common with the local woods, meadows and lanes as a place where I had an absolute right to go to play. Of all of them however, the station was the main attraction. There always seemed to be so much to watch and take part in.

The station, I suppose, was typical of many hundreds of local English country stations. To me though it possessed a

"The railway clock ticked away comfortably as if it would go on for ever"

certain grandeur that some of its neighbours did not. Blocks of building on each side of the line supported a glass canopy over the platform. They housed offices, store rooms, toilets and waiting rooms, including one general and one for ladies. In winter there would be a fire burning in the open fireplace, above which the standard round railway clock ticked away slowly and comfortably as though it would go on for ever.

Next to the main door was a large weighing machine with sliding weights on a bar. We children used it as the imaginary footplate for our locomotive, aided by the genuine sound effects from outside.

Children were not allowed into the booking office – or hardly ever. Occasionally in the evening when I went to the station alone, Joe - the warehouseman-cum-porter, who seemed to be as permanent as the station itself – permitted me to enter. I felt highly privileged as I examined the racks of cardboard tickets, mysterious ledgers, pots containing small change and the ambulance box. By the fire which always seemed to be burning there was a chair upholstered with horsehair. The stuffing was bursting out and made a

prickly seat for a boy in short trousers.

Quite often to curry favour I would collect coal that had fallen from wagons on to the track or been spilled in the goods yard. Sometimes I was even allowed to stamp a ticket in the little cylindrical

machine used for this purpose. It meant sliding the ticket between the metal lips of the machine and pushing it briskly. A satisfying click indicated that it had been properly stamped. There was a knack to it but I was usually so excited and nervous that my efforts would turn out miserable failures and Joe would have to do them over again.

I remember pushing up the wooden shutter on the box office window and feeling the wooden counter worn smooth through years of transactions. There was even a depression in the floorboards outside this window where so many people had stood to receive their tickets.

On dark winter evenings I would help in lighting the station gas lamps. Joe would lift me up in the waiting room so I could pull the chain which lit the lamps with a plop and a rush of bright light. On the platforms under the canopies there were three or four lights with mantles contained in what looked like squat test tubes with a hole in the bottom. We had to go round with a long pole to light these.

Joe seemed to me to have the best job in the world. He could book tickets, use the crane, turn the goods yard points - there was nothing he couldn't do! Best of all he knew how much I loved these things too and he would often let me, though explaining what trouble he would be in if we were discovered by the station master.

In time I also learnt the secrets of the signal box: the bell code and which levers operated which points. I was even allowed to turn the large ship's wheel which operated the crossing gates.

But the ultimate joy was those special days when a good natured driver would allow me to clamber up into his cab and join him on the footplate. It seemed so easy to drive an engine. You just pushed up or pulled down a single lever. Sometimes I would be allowed to drive the engine down to Charles Moore's salt works to pick up a couple of salt vans. It was only about three hundred yards but what ecstasy could be packed into half an hour on the footplate! Each steam engine

seemed to have its own personality. Just to watch the locomotive passing by was a fascination, but to feel the vibration under one's feet as the engine took up its load, to feel the heat of the fire box as the door was opened for stoking and to hear the clank of the wheels as the train gathered speed were delights only to be fully enjoyed from the footplate.

Today only the shells of the buildings remain, while the atmosphere, smells, sights and sounds of the railway have disappeared for ever. It is sad to think that no small boy will ever again experience the excitement and pleasures of Heatley station that filled my childhood.

"On dark winter evenings I would help in lighting the station gas lamps"

A businessman, a factory worker, two ladies and a family. The railways brought a new democracy to travel though some opted for first class even from Heatley to Lymm.

WHAT HAPPENED NEXT
down at
HEATLEY & WARBURTON

These three pictures were taken from almost the same location—looking toward the site of the level crossing on Mill Lane.

In the top picture, taken just after the Second World War the platform on the left still has its imposing glass canopy so fondly remembered by Roy Holt.

By the late 1950s—the second picture, this has gone as has half of the cover on the other platform. Most noticeable perhaps is that there is not a soul to be seen on either photograph.

And today … The remains of the building are the only physical reminder of the age of the railway in Lymm. The only wheels turning on this track now are bicycles.

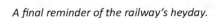

A final reminder of the railway's heyday.

A REAL "EL DORADO"

The railway opened up Lymm to commercial travellers and the enterprising Mr Milnes of Youngs, who dealt in candles, oil, lamps and chimneys, used the railway to reach his customers and, on one memorable occasion, employed the Ship Canal to deliver his goods.

"It was about the middle of the month of September 1874, a beautiful crispy morning with just a slight touch of frost in the air. When I alighted from the train and breathed the salubrious atmosphere of Lymm, if I had any misgivings on the way as to my reception by the good people whom I had to visit, they were quickly dispelled, for the invigorating atmospheric conditions and the beautiful foliage just putting on its Autumn tints, made me think I had drifted into a veritable Garden of Eden. However away I sped to the village, and noted all its antiquity – the Cross, the Stocks and the crescent of shops all appearing to be doing well, in fact I felt I had come to a real El Dorado."

Mr Milne's products were widely sold and sought after, from Henshalls the Chemist (now Sextons bakery) to Mr Whitelegge the grocer and, facing the cross, Mr Taylor the ironmonger.

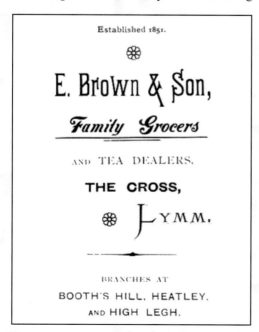

"..I had drifted into a veritable Garden of Eden .."

Shortly after the opening of the Ship Canal in 1894 Mr Milnes landed a big order with E. Brown & Sons of Lymm for their new long burning halfpenny wax candles that would be a boon to local fustian cutters. Mr Brown felt sure that they would be a big seller. Accordingly, to create a sensation, he ordered one hundred cases to be delivered in a single consignment. Mr Milnes, seeing an opportunity for some great publicity arranged for them to be offloaded at the new Ship Canal passenger jetty in Statham. They were carted to the village with the sides of the vehicle proudly proclaiming them to be the first delivery to Lymm via the new Ship Canal. The unloading created quite a stir that drew the attention of the local constable. However, he was less than sympathetic to their publicity efforts - and promptly booked them for obstruction!

Glazebrook Station as realised by members of **Warrington Model Railway Society** at **Lymm Historic Transport Day.**

The station forms part of a line from Liverpool to Manchester that was built by the Cheshire Lines Committee at the very end of the railway building era in 1873.

It became the third rail link between Liverpool and Manchester.

The first was the northern link based on the route originally used by Stephenson's Rocket—world's first twin-track inter-urban passenger railway in which all the trains were timetabled and ticketed.

The second was the L &NWR route that served Lymm.

Three routes between two cities was always going to be a competitive challenge and the Lymm line was sadly the first to succumb. The other two remain open.

RIGHT: Down line freight at Glazebrook 1957.

Warrington Model Railway Society's
Exhibition was one of the hits of Historic
Transport Day and their layouts certainly
embraced the broader transport theme of
the event.
Kinwardine Wharf (right and bottom
right) and Stockton Mill were just two of
the layouts on display that were authentic
down to the very minutest detail including
the colouring and lettering on the working
canal boats.

To get an idea of the scale they were working to, look at the hand in the top picture.

Ships Across the Fields

THE MANCHESTER SHIP CANAL

A WITTY LETTER TO A LIVERPOOL NEWSPAPER IN 1825 suggested that the corporation should send a representative to a dinner of the Manchester Canal shareholders in 1825 and, when they were in good humour having eaten and drunk well, to read them a poem which started:

Oh ye Lords of the loom
Pray avert our sad doom
We humbly beseech on our knees
We do not complain
That you drink your champagne
But leave us our port if you please.

The letter was a reference to the Corporation's anxiety about a proposal that had gone before Parliament in the previous year to construct a canal from the Dee Estuary through Frodsham, Lymm and Didsbury into Manchester - effectively by-passing Liverpool.

In the end the bill was vigorously opposed by any number of interested parties and thrown out. The burghers of Liverpool breathed a huge sigh of relief; for another two generations anyway.

An increasingly rare sight since the 1960s. A ship across the fields— This picture was taken from Ridgeway-Grundy Park across the rooftops of Statham Close and was one of the Manchester Liners fleet.

This scheme was one of a series dating back to the early 18th century aimed at making Manchester more accessible to shipping. The existing Mersey & Irwell route had always seemed to offer the most feasible prospect of achieving this, and in 1734 a project was completed to build a series of locks and so improve navigation. It included the Butchersfield Canal which cut out a huge loop of the river that came close to Statham. Vestiges of this can still be seen at Lymm Golf Club. However, the Mersey & Irwell solution was always a compromise. It was subject to the vagaries of the weather and could only take small vessels.

Soon after the bill failed in 1825, attention switched to Rainhill and to the Liverpool to Manchester Railway which opened five years later. Any idea of promoting new canals was put on the back burner as rail mania gripped the nation. But in the 1880s, as the scale of industry grew, so the demand for the cheap movement of heavy goods such as timber and cotton grew with it. The Mersey & Irwell waterway had fallen into decline

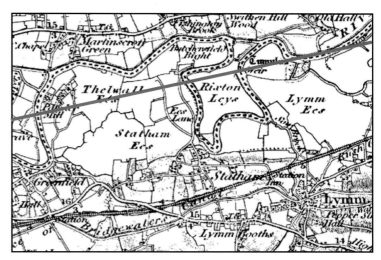

The map shows just how close the Mersey used to come to Statham. The name may well originate from the old Norse Stathe-ham—meaning the settlement by the landing place. The straight blue line indicates approximately how the canal cut through leaving sections of the river stranded.

and disrepair with the arrival, first of the Bridgewater Canal, then the railways. A meeting held at the home of Daniel Adamson in 1882 was the final catalyst for the building of the great new waterway and was the first step to gaining Royal Assent in 1885.

The canal was a vast undertaking. Much was done by manual labour though steam excavators were used and the project benefited from the huge strides in civil engineering made during the period of "railway mania" in the previous fifty years. This picture was taken near Warrington.

The old and the new. Thelwall Ferry across the Ship Canal with the M6 behind. At just 12p to cross to the other side it's great value! The nearby pontoon bridge was abandoned after an accident when two horses drowned in the 1940s but the ferry, which is sculled by local man Kevin Wilkinson, still carries 600 passengers a year. The motorway in the background carries rather more.

By the time the first sod of the Manchester Ship Canal was turned in 1887, Lymm must have been at fever pitch in anticipation of such a huge project taking place on its doorstep. This canal would not cut through the village like the Bridgewater had 130 years before, but the scale of the undertaking was vast and beyond any engineering project ever previously tackled in this country.

The canal would cut a mighty swathe through the landscape and would even move boundaries. Part of Statham was to be isolated on the north bank and it eventually left Cheshire to become part of Lancashire. In nearby Thelwall a farm was divided and a deal was made for the canal company to provide a pontoon bridge that would allow the farmer to access his land with a horse and cart on the other bank using a windlass. To this day there is a ferry service on the site.

The canal must have been the topic of much lively conversation on the morning train from Lymm to Manchester. Among the regular passengers were Mr Alfred Watkin who had a senior role with one of the canal contractors and Mr Boumphrey of Baycliffe whose cotton business would certainly have prospered as a result of the canal . The talk may have turned to the local changes that would result from the building of the waterway and the idea of taking the opportunity to build a golf course on its banks was born. The nine hole course was opened in 1907.

It was another statement about the changing character of the village, though the proximity of a sewage filled canal may not always have made for the most pleasant playing conditions in the early days.

Itinerant hot drink sellers did a roaring trade along the canal. These navvies are having a break outside their huts

The biggest local impact on the village from 1887 was the number of migrant labourers and their families who arrived to work on the construction. Some took up lodgings in Lymm and Oughtrington. Temporary shanty towns also sprang up including one between Warburton and Statham. It consisted of three long streets with twenty wooden huts in each. Walter Struthers recalled his parents once living in one of the more permanent wooden buildings which had been constructed for foremen, on the site of what is now Lymmington Avenue. The influx caused quite an upheaval at Oughtrington School too. In March 1888 the headmaster Mr Goldsmith wrote in his journal:

" admitted several new boys whose fathers have found employment at Ship Canal works. The specimens I have had so far are not very satisfactory and are rather migratory in their habits"

By April 1889 his opinion had not changed:

"I find the children of the Ship Canal labourers to be most unsatisfactory in every way —loose in their attendance, untidy and unkempt and as a rule most backward in work"

But poor work and attendance were the least of their worries in Oughtrington at the time. Between making these two entries the scarlet fever which had plagued the area for many years struck a triple blow at the headmaster's own family. He lost two children within hours of each other and a third the day after their funeral.

There were regular tragedies down at the canal too, including many deaths on just the Lymm section of the excavation. In 1890 the newspapers reported:

"Young Mr Griffiths met with a shocking death on Thursday afternoon. He was stooping behind a stationary wagon to pick up a piece of iron when another wagon came down an adjoining line, and jumping off the rails at the point where Griffiths was, jammed his head against the buffers of the stationary wagon. The unfortunate youth's head was smashed and death was instantaneous. The body was conveyed to the hospital at Thelwall where the inquest will be held today. ..."

Explosives were yet another deadly hazard. On one occasion a gang of men were at work on the Lymm section, drilling holes for dynamite blasting. Having filled seven and believing they had detonated them all the men returned to their boat. A sudden unexpected explosion shook the area and one of the men was killed instantly. Three more were seriously injured and were rushed to hospital at Latchford. The newspaper report added ominously *"they are not expected to live."*

But all the dramas and tragedies that had accompanied the building of the canal were swept aside as towns and villages along the route turned out to celebrate its opening. Commercial traffic from the Mersey started on New Year's day January 1894 though boats had already been travelling on the Lymm stretch for three years. This created the strange vision of large ships appearing to glide across the fields. Within days the first vessels from distant ports like New Orleans were passing along the northern edge of Lymm.

RIGHT: The very first steamer from New Orleans in January 1894 unloading 4,300 bales of cotton in the new Port of Manchester. It would have been an awe inspiring and unfamiliar sight across the fields from Lymm.

The sound of regular explosions would have been heard all over the area as rock was blasted away. This was just one of many hazards. It was recognised from the outset that there would be many casualties during construction and a chain of temporary hospitals was built along the route of which the nearest to Lymm was at Thelwall.

There were ships on the canal three years before Queen Victoria's visit though the access to the Mersey estuary was only opened on January 1st 1894.

Mary Ann Seymour (née Read) was ten when the canal was officially opened on May 21st 1894 by Queen Victoria. Mary had already heard a lot about it from her father who walked every day from their cottage at the bottom of Sandy Lane to work on its construction. She was one of nine children and on the day of the opening her school on Pepper Street had a holiday. The children tramped across the fields together to get a view of the parade of boats as it passed. Mary never got to see the Queen who came no nearer than Salford but she always remembered the colourful procession.

The canal continued to touch her family's life. Her father was employed as a maintenance man engaged in constant repairs to the sides of the canal. Within a few months of the opening Mary's own life changed forever when she left school, aged eleven, to work in a fustian cutting shop in Fletcher's Lane.

The canal would certainly not have been universally welcomed. It represented a massive upheaval to the lives of people whose homes were close by. In the year that the Lymm section opened the Manchester papers carried this distressing report.

"A farmer at Statham, near Lymm named Joseph Tickle was found at seven on Tuesday morning in his calf cote with his throat cut. He had a carving knife in his hand. His wife had noticed his strange manner and went to look for him. She noticed him lying down and gave an alarm. Although the body was warm he was quite dead".

Whilst we will never know for certain what had driven the farmer to such despair there is no doubt that the coming of the canal would have been traumatic.

From the very beginning the canal was also carrying a new cargo – people. The Manchester Passenger Steam Company was formed in 1893 in anticipation of this great new business opportunity. From January 2nd 1894 passenger boats were running from Manchester direct to Liverpool. But there was another potential source of business, the day-tripper from Manchester for whom Liverpool was too far.

Lymm was an obvious landing-place. It could be reached on a day's round trip from Manchester and already had a reputation as an attractive destination for cyclists and rail passengers. Work began quickly on a landing stage at Statham and it was ready by May 1894. The opening of the new jetty was announced in the Manchester Courier:

"The Ship Canal Passenger Steam Company Limited have just completed the erection of landing stages on the canal for the use of their steamers at Eccles and Lymm. The stage at Lymm will prove a great boon to many as direct access will thereby be given to one of the most attractive spots in the vicinity of the canal. The village of Lymm is only three-quarters of a mile from the canal and has always been a popular resort for excursion parties."

The Passenger Company would have been keen to be operating by Whitsun which was one of the busiest weekends for trippers. There were several boats servicing the route including Clyde paddle steamers that had been repositioned to take advantage of this great new enterprise. The public were quick to respond and by the following year the company reported in the press that they had brought a staggering 16,000 people to Lymm, Barton and Eccles over the Whitsun holiday

There was no shortage of attractions at The Star Inn on Star Lane

alone. Quite what they did when they arrived is less certain. The description of the village as being "three-quarters of a mile from the canal" is surely poetic licence. Some of the boats had just a one hour turn round at Lymm and it would have been a very brisk walk to the village and back in that time. A picnic in the farmer's field or a refreshing pint at the Star on Barsbank Lane was a more realistic goal.

Statham Jetty probably 1894 or 1895—the boat's name is unfortunately indistinguishable. The picture was taken by Pel Ardern, photographer, of Eagle Brow.

Just as quickly as the passenger steamers appeared they seem to have vanished. Word may have got around that the three hour trip to Lymm, half of it through an industrial landscape, actually got you nowhere near the centre of the village. Lymm could be reached more cheaply and far more quickly by train, wagonette or even bicycle. At least one of the packet boats, The Daniel Adamson (quickly renamed from "Shandon" to honour the main sponsor of the canal), returned to the Clyde at the end of the 1895 season destined for the breaker's yard.

Another negative may have been what started as a bad smell and quickly became an appalling stink. Back in Salford and Manchester the canal had become an outlet for sewerage. By 1899 it had become intolerable.

Advertisement for Ship Canal cruises –1895

The Vicar of Thelwall described the stench as unbearable for his congregation particularly in summer and when a steamer passed and churned up the *"sickening effluvium"*. A mile or two away people in Lymm were threatening to give up possession of their property, such was their distress. In 1891 untreated sewage from a population of one and a half million came pouring down the Mersey and the Ship Canal. By 1899 this had been greatly reduced but by then the damage was done. With a problem like that then a paddle steamer was probably not the ideal form of transport. As late as the 1960s people who lived near the canal were still complaining of the smell from passing boats on a warm summer's day.

Once the passenger boats had gone, the canal barely touched people's lives in Lymm. For most residents the main reminder of its existence was the constant opening and closing of Latchford Bridge for those aiming to visit Warrington. Shipping volumes increased up to the 1950s followed by a steady decline. They peaked in 1958 at over 20 million tons, and Manchester Liners converted four ships to container vessels in the 1960s. These were the largest users of the canal but the increasing size of ocean-going ships and Salford Port's failure to introduce modern freight-handling methods resulted in that headline figure dropping steadily, and ended with the closure of the docks in Salford in 1984.

Latchford Locks 1958- The peak year for Ship Canal Traffic. Just one bicycle on the road but work would start on the Thelwall Viaduct within the year. It was built at a height to accommodate ships but ironically contributed to the canal's decline as more and more freights moved to the roads.

Statham late 1950s—the small rowing boat was used to access the pumping station on the other side but was also commandeered by children to sit in .

The banks of the canal were a magnet as a playground for the adventurous. Alan Taylor recalls the excitement as a child of exploring the abandoned concrete barges that still rest to this day on a backwater at Statham that was once the Mersey. There were plenty of ships to watch sailing by. The more daring amongst them would sit on a small rowing boat to ride out the wash from passing ships. Tugs returning on their own from an assignment were particularly impressive in this respect. The water was still foul though and often covered with a coating of fuel oil. Just throwing in a lighted cigarette could cause an explosion and in one case, in the 1960s, a fatal sinking of the local ferry at nearby Partington.

The new waterway did in one sense serve to redefine the people of Lymm along with Thelwall, Grappenhall and Stockton Heath as the folk "south of the canal" especially when Lymm became part of the Borough of Warrington in 1974. Some have even argued that the canal represents the furthest possible north limit of the north/south divide with industrial Lancashire above it and agricultural Cheshire below. These days there is far less commercial traffic – though Peel Holdings has ambitious plans. As in so many places now tourism is one of the main industries with regular cruises the whole length of the waterway –a six hour journey. The sounds of ships' engines and hooters have been replaced by the amplified voice of a tour guide retelling the amazing story of the building of "The Big Ditch".

All aboard The Snowdrop.

These days a cruise along the length of The Ship Canal has a positively continental feel about it compared to the sewage stirring journeys of the nineteenth century. This picture was taken just east of Warburton Bridge in September 2013 with the short severed arm of the Mersey in the foreground.

THE LOCOMOTIVE "LYMM"

The building of the Ship Canal involved the creation of a huge web of 230 miles of railway, working its way in and out, over and under and alongside every point of construction. The lines were used by 173 locomotives and 6,300 sturdy seven ton wagons. The custom on this project, as it had been on the Bridgewater Canal, was to name new vehicles after the parishes along the route. "Lymm" was built by the Hunslet Company of Leeds and completed in 1888 by which time canal building had already started. After less than three years her work on the canal was done and she was sold on to be part of another huge project.

The Lancashire Derbyshire and East Coast Railway was the largest railway scheme ever approved by Parliament in a single session. The plan was to connect the new Ship Canal from docks at Warrington to the East Coast with the route passing through Lymm, Prestbury and Macclesfield, and on through the Derbyshire coalfields to the east coast at Sutton on Sea. The Act was passed in 1891 and was to be one of the very last major new rail lines. In the end work came to a halt after the completion of the Chesterfield to Lincoln section and "Lymm" was once more in search of work.

In 1896 she was sold to a quarrying company in the Rossendale valley and finally ended her working life as late as 1947 in another quarry near Facit in Lancashire. After that she was left in a shed and largely forgotten except by train tourists until she was finally dragged out in October 1959 and, like so many other steam engines at the time, broken up. She had retained her nameplate till the very end.

The driver and his team stop work briefly at Ince in around 1890 though one of them obviously found it difficult to stand still !

Pedalling History

A QUIET REVOLUTION FOR THE WORKING MAN AND WOMAN

T HE SADDLE OF A BICYCLE was, in the view of most gentlemen riders of the 1880s "no place for a lady".

The boneshaker had started to appear in the 1860s. It was the preserve of the affluent and possibly slightly eccentric gentleman. This primitive machine offered a very uncomfortable ride and had little to commend it for a journey of any distance particularly given the state of the roads. It was quickly replaced in the 1870s by the high-wheel, more commonly known now as the penny-farthing. This was no more suitable for female riders in view of the immodest riding position and so for another ten years the men had the highways to themselves. It was the safety cycle, developed in the 1880s, so called apparently because it was actually safe to fall off, that finally opened up the bicycle to the wider population including women.

Lymm May Queen 1907 in Elm Tree Road looking toward Church Road and the Temperance Hotel that offered "large rooms for cyclists". It looks as if some female visitors are taking advantage of the view.

In the last ten years of the nineteenth century the craze for cycling gathered momentum. Clubs were formed, and newspapers carried regular features on the joys of cycling that described exciting day trips to destinations like Rostherne, Lymm, Bowdon and Pickmere. By the Edwardian era cycling had entered its "mania" phase. Prices were coming down as mass production got under way and the bicycle offered a new independence and companionship for the working man and woman.

Richardson's—Motor & Cycle Oils. Many shops had their own distinctive smell too. This one apparently acquired its own from a mix of paraffin, lubricating oil and rubber.

This photograph at the top of Eagle Brow may have been prompted by the kittens but Mrs Greenman was not going to miss the opportunity to show off her new bicycle.

The bicycle offered new opportunities for commerce too. The Temperance Hotel on Church Road in Lymm offered large rooms for cyclists. Tea rooms and cycle shops opened in large numbers, at one time Lymm had no fewer than five of the latter. Some of the Lymm businesses such as Holt's Café at the Dingle and Richardson's Cycles opposite the Golden Fleece

became an established part of the local scene for many decades. As with every new craze not everyone saw it as a positive. In some places cyclists appeared in their hundreds and certain villages felt that the large numbers of riders disturbed the even tenor of their ways. Over in Knutsford, Lord Egerton who had reaped the rewards of the Industrial Revolution through, among other things, his involvement with the Manchester Ship Canal was certainly not impressed when the industrial workforce took to the roads to escape the grimy and polluted environs of places like Manchester and Salford to "invade" his pastoral domain.

1929—It was Sunday so some of the men still felt compelled to wear a tie.

By 1910 more motor-cars were also starting to appear but they would for many years remain well beyond the pocket of the working man or woman. Instead the bicycle represented emancipation and liberation. This theme was picked up by the Clarion movement, a nationwide socialist group whose motto was "Fellowship is Life". Clubs sprang up all over the country for sports, drama, rambling and, most successfully, cycling. They would organise rides and often take the opportunity to give out socialist leaflets at their chosen destination. The Bolton club often came to Lymm and in 1929 they assembled at the Cross for a team picture. There is no record of whether this was just a pleasure trip or if there was an element of "missionary work".

The Bolton branch is in existence to this day. They still call regularly at Lymm, attracted apparently by the new wave of tea rooms, and in 2011 they reassembled at the Cross for another group photograph in remembrance of that club ride over eighty years earlier..

2011—Bolton Clarion Club, the Lycra generation.
These days they ride with no political affiliation.

In earlier days Lymm's many hostelries would have been another attraction. As well as The Golden Fleece, The Spread Eagle and The Bull's Head - which are all still open today - there was the Bridgewater looking onto the canal near the present day Youth & Community Centre and the Millstone facing the corn mill, next to the mill manager's cottage on the lower dam; all now sadly gone. The two cyclists in the picture below look very much like post-boys whose job included making express deliveries of telegrams.

After the Second World War many bicycles were consigned to the shed or the scrapheap as the working man fell in love with the motor car. Cycling was seen as the territory of the less well-off and also became less a pleasure and more an ordeal due to the huge increase in car and lorry traffic.

But by the time the last coal train had rattled through Lymm in 1985, cycling was enjoying a new wave of

Lymm —still a popular destination for cyclists

popularity as more and more people became disillusioned with motoring for pleasure. There was a growing awareness of the environmental impact of motor transport to which cycling was the perfect antidote. In 1989 the concept of a long distance path from west to east coast was born and the disused railway line running through Lymm offered an obvious opportunity to create part of the route.

he corner at the lower dam was very congested and involved a very
harp turn that would have been impractical for modern traffic.
regson's mill is just visible, left. The mill manager's house on the right
as designed to derive maximum benefit from the view.

A distinctive signpost on the Trans-Pennine Trail at Lymm

Today it forms a section of the Trans Pennine Trail from Southport in the west to Hornsea in the east; a distance of over 200 miles. The Lymm stretch of the trail even forms a part of the longer E8 European long distance path. So remember, if you go down to the Rangers' hut near the Lymm Hotel, turn left for Cork and right for Istanbul.

There have been two further celebrations of cycling in Lymm recently. In September 2012, the Tour of Britain came through the edge of the village for the first time ever and the eagle eyed had the opportunity, momentarily, to see cycling heroes Bradley Wiggins and Mark Cavendish sweep past in a blur of lycra and titanium.

And in June 2013 cycling enthusiasts had a great opportunity to see a fabulous collection of bicycles through the ages provided by the Veteran Cycle Club at **Lymm Historic Transport Day.**

Yes it really happened .. In 2012 Mark Cavendish and Bradley Wiggins were national heroes , World and Olympic champions respectively when they raced through Lymm in September 2012.

BELOW: and this is where it all started. Chris Hocking's 1888 solid tyred safety bicycle at Historic Transport Day.

The Veteran Cycle Club entering into the spirit of Historic Transport Day in costume and music as well providing a great display of historic cycles.

From TOP LEFT CLOCKWISE

Everyone's favourite–
The penny-farthing or more precisely an 1881 Humber Ordinary belonging to Ian Dunning.
Mike Walker blowing the VCC trumpet.
Gordon Blakie in pensive mood.
Chris & Joan entertained us.
A sample of the bikes on show.

A TRIP FROM MANCHESTER TO LYMM

Newspapers at the end of nineteenth century had tapped into "cycling mania" with descriptions of day trips to attractive destinations. These pieces tended to be low on hard fact and high on "gush" but nevertheless they provide a rare insight into the village scene 120 years ago. The opening sentences of this article from **The Manchester Weekly Times** of 1893 hint that the even tenor of village life is starting to be unsettled by the number of visitors; and while there is much vivid description of nature's bounty, one senses a certain wink and a nod toward the pleasures of the pub too. The reference to "the odorous Mersey" is prescient. Just six years later residents of Statham would be threatening to leave their homes, overwhelmed by the stench from the new Ship Canal.

As the eye wanders it rests upon many evidences of the bustling and abundant life of to-day. The numerous conveyances passing to and fro laden with joyous pleasure seekers; the many cycles leaning with modest unobtrusiveness against the walls of "pubs", as if protesting that they are they are there by mere accident, their owners have not gone inside but slipped round the corner to replenish their oil-cans; the carts laden with goods or with the "kindly fruits of the earth" and drawn by very sleek and well-fed horses; all these combine to give this old world village, with its half-timbered and red-brick cottages a most delightful and poetic charm. Though that unscrupulous vandal, the modern builder, has made encroachments here, and dotted many a piece of raw and glaring brickwork amid the mellow lichen-stained and grey and russet productions of time; yet this comingling of ancient and modern, of the rusticity of a past age with the prim

Lymm
from the canal —

pretentiousness of the present has failed to spoil the primitive beauty of the place.

Leaving our quiet "mounts" in charge of mine host of the Fleece Hotel we proceed to visit those spots which nature and art together have combined to make Lymm supremely lovely. Through the village runs a tiny stream, the Dane, which for about three miles above has wended its way through a romantic valley, the lower part of which is thickly wooded with an undergrowth of elder and briar, honeysuckle and bramble. A considerable portion of this charming vale has been converted into a large and placidly beautiful lake by damming up the waters of the stream. On the right side begins the walk down "The Hollow" which is so justly famed. The overflow water from the lake descends the moss crowned stone steps into the dell below, and though at this time of midsummer drought it is but a slight, silvery trickle, there are times when, after a sudden storm the waters tumble down, white and voiceful and impressive. Along this dingle walk wherever the eye turns the view is very pleasing. Trees embower your

church which together from a group sufficiently full of picturesque beauty to rouse the soul of the artist to the wildest enthusiasm. The stream creeps from beneath

valley, possibly of volcanic origin, comes to an abrupt end and the Dane runs on through lush meadows until it loses itself in the odorous Mersey.

By this time the sun is sinking and we are warned that it would be prudent to depart. Having strongly fortified the inner man we trim and light our lamps, affix them and soon we are bowling along with our faces homeward turned. Winged things flit ghost-like past us. A benighted hare darts from the hedge-side, hirples up the road and a hedgehog slowly crossing our path nearly falls victim to its temerity. The lights of the great city come more and more prominently into view and presently our day's run is numbered with the pleasant things that have been".

Lymm Cheshire

walking, overhead a green canopy through which, here and there, the sun's rays fall like columns of transparent gold. Ferns, lichens and creepers and wild flowers innumerable carpet the moist earth, and the tiny runlet murmurs soothingly in the ear.

Passing the lower dam through the village, we climb the canal embankment through the village near the flatman's haven of rest, the Bridgewater Arms. Here, near the bridge of the Bridgewater Canal our artist takes up his stand to sketch the mill, the bridge and the distant

the sombre shadow of the bridge at the lower dam. On the left is Gregson's corn mill and nearer are gardens from whence arises the mingled perfume of many sweet flowers, sweet william, tiger lily, hollyhock and marigold. Troops of butterflies chase each other from flower to flower and there is a murmur of bees in the air.

Continuing along Whitbarrow Lane rocks rise high on either side. The Dane widens. Still lower down is another waterfall equal in beauty to those on the upper reaches and shortly afterward this long

The artist, Hedley Fitton, who was born in Didsbury in 1859 trained at The Warrington School of Art. After a spell with Manchester newspapers he travelled widely and went on to become an eminent engraver and printmaker noted mainly for his architectural etchings. He exhibited at the Royal Academy and the Paris Salon.

THE ASTONISHING TALE OF THE
INVASION OF ROSTHERNE

Improvements in transport didn't just bring easier travel for people living in the village. They also provided access for all to places like Lymm, Thelwall, Pickmere and Rostherne which could now be reached on a day trip. They came in their thousands, though gradually at first. Toward the end of the eighteenth century they arrived on packet boat trips along the Bridgewater Canal. In the second half

Intrepid cyclists took to the roads in their hundreds and even thousands to escape the choking grime of the industrial towns. This group were sketched in 1896 passing through Thelwall.

of the nineteenth century they came on railway excursions from Manchester. And by the end of the century there was a whole new wave of visitors – sixteen thousand at Whitsun weekend in 1895

who sailed along the Ship Canal on trip boats to the new jetty at Statham.

By the turn of the twentieth century road access was improving too. Newspapers from surrounding areas extolled the pleasures of Lymm for the keen cyclist and a little later they were joined and eventually outnumbered by motorists leaving great clouds of dust behind them

as they ploughed along the unmetalled tracks at speeds up to the limit of 20 mph.

Press articles may have described the joys of the countryside and the architecture of

the churches, but to judge from the local news reports many visitors were rather more interested in the opportunity to relax after a hard week's work with a few beers at one of Lymm's many hostelries.

In 1903 the chair of the local Lymm magistrates observed that:

"extra staff of police had to be kept at Lymm on Sunday to look after the cyclists and motorists".

Arley May Festival had already been forced to abandon their simple annual ceremony on the village green because of unruly visitors. The same reason was given by Lord Stamford for closing Dunham Park to the public.

Clearly these *"hordes of cyclists"* were seen by some in Edwardian days as an even bigger menace than the motor car. Down the road, in Rostherne, things were taking a more confrontational turn with the great "No Teas in Rostherne" showdown of 1909. The village was by then one of the most popular destinations for cyclists, so it was no great surprise when villagers took the opportunity to eke out their meagre income by selling jugs of tea to the day-trippers. Lord Egerton was determined to do something about what he saw as an unwelcome invasion and he forbade his tenants from trading with trippers on pain of eviction. When news spread of the ban, cyclists and ramblers poured in from near and far to protest.

Rostherne Church

And two weeks later they were back in their thousands again. But this time there was a special force of police ready for them and they found the church field, where they planned to meet, closed to them. They eventually gathered in the school playground where there were speeches by Labour and Liberal MPs. Among the cyclists there would almost certainly have been members of the many socialist Clarion Clubs.

A resolution of protest was passed but Lord Egerton did not make himself available to accept it. His spokesperson Mr Crossley challenged the protestors.

"They should go to the inns" he declared and was immediately reminded that he was treasurer of The United Kingdom Alliance – a teetotal organisation.

The effects of the conflict can be seen to this day. Rostherne is now a village without pubs—closed down by Lord Egerton to deter "those unwelcome visitors".

"Fully 10,000 cyclists invaded Rostherne on Saturday amid scenes of unprecedented character"

The Knutsford Guardian of May 12 1909 reported:

"Fully 10,000 cyclists, many motorists and hundreds of pedestrians invaded the village of Rostherne on Saturday. Scenes of unprecedented character, in this part of Cheshire at any rate, were witnessed. The object of the demonstration was to protest at Lord Egerton's having forbidden his tenantry to supply visitors except on pains of being compelled to immediately quit their homesteads ..."

Cycling clubs attracted huge memberships. This is Bolton Clarion Club. There are nearly 700 people in this picture. There were 10,000 at Rostherne that day ..plus bicycles

That Intolerable Nuisance

THE COMING OF THE MOTOR CAR

AT THE TURN OF THE CENTURY LYMM WAS STRUGGLING TO COPE with the frequent weekend invasion of visitors. In addition to the bicycles there were regular day-trip trains from Manchester and Warrington. The launch of Manchester Ship Canal passenger excursions to Statham in 1894 simply added to the numbers.

However it was motorists who quickly came to be seen as the biggest problem. In 1903 magistrates came down hard on a local driver who was arrested for dangerous driving in excess of twelve mph (the speed limit) on Booths Hill Road and for failing to sound his gong (yes, that's right: *gong*) when overtaking. It is easy to imagine though that he would have been gripping the wheel hard with both hands while attempting to complete this hair-raising manoeuvre on the poorly surfaced road.

Local police were determined to stamp down on this *"furious driving"* and extra officers were on the streets of Lymm at weekends to keep cyclists and motorists under some sort of control.

A new century and a new era in transport. On this early coloured postcard a car makes a first appearance, adding a touch of affluence and sophistication to the scene.

The country as a whole was waking up to the fact that the car was here to stay even if at this stage it was still the rich man's plaything. Quite who owned the very first car in Lymm is a matter of some debate. George Fairclough who lived on the corner of Barsbank Lane in 1902 is one candidate. These were still primitive vehicles and it was not unusual for his car to be towed home by horse. Mr Watkin of Danebank and

There is no surviving picture of Mr Boumphrey at the wheel of his Wolseley-Siddeley but this is the model he drove.

Note the large folding hood, yet no sign of a windscreen for it to latch on to. The starting handle protrudes out from the nearside of the car, rather than the front, with the chain drive to the rear wheels visible also. The car has two acetylene lamps fitted to the scuttle, yet only one large main lamp up front, on the offside.

Mr Boumphrey of Baycliffe who collaborated in the building of Lymm's golf course were also two of the very early pioneers. Mr Boumphrey drove a 1905 Wolseley-Siddeley. The early car owners were inevitably the wealthiest members of the community. Doctors too were among the first to acquire cars and in Lymm that was Dr Thorp. All these pioneers may have been inspired by the much publicised motoring

trials organised by the Liverpool Self-Propelled Traffic Association which came through Lymm each year from 1899 until 1901.

If the roads weren't really ready to cope with cars then neither it would seem were the drivers. As a result there were many accidents like this one caused by visitors from Manchester and reported in the local press in 1907

"A car was descending Church Green, the hill leading into the village from the direction of the Manchester Road when, on approaching the cross in the market-place, the driver appeared to be in two minds which way to go. In the end he turned rather sharply. A wheel of the car collapsed and the car turned completely over trapping two people underneath."

Fortunately no-one was killed. The driver and his passengers were taken to a nearby cottage where they were treated by a local doctor.

Mrs Holden, another member of the Boumphrey family, certainly had the pioneer spirit when it came to transport. As well as becoming a volunteer ambulance driver in the First World War she toured Scotland by motorbike in 1922 on a 3.5Hhp Martindale.

After the First World War with mass production getting under way more and more deliveries were made by "horseless vehicles". In this case it is a steam wagon; the chimney is clearly visible coming up through the cab. The driver and his mates are posing in front of The Church Green. Behind them the wagon is loaded with vital supplies of Wilderspool Ales from the brewery in Warrington.

Sometimes it was an adventurous local driver who would end up in trouble. In 1908 Tom Gregson, who ran the mill at the lower dam and the bakery on Eagle Brow, drove all the way to Southport, quite a feat in itself. Unfortunately for him his day finished in a police cell when he was stopped on the promenade and arrested, not for the first time, for being "the worse for drink".

Stories like these serve to illustrate just how unprepared the country was for the burgeoning number of vehicles on the road. Cars had no indicators or windscreen wipers and their lights were very poor. There was no instruction and there would be no driving test for another thirty years. The roads themselves were still atrocious and made worse by the increasing numbers of cars. In dry weather they created great dust clouds up to forty feet high while in wet conditions they cut deep ruts into the roads.

By 1912 local residents had had enough and were protesting to the local council, though there must have been the feeling that they were fighting a losing battle. Lymm Council in turn instructed the clerk to write to the President of the Local Government Board calling attention to:

" the great nuisance caused by the swift motor car driving especially to cottagers whose houses abut on the highway. With a hope that something will be done at once to prevent this intolerable nuisance"

It is hard to imagine what this letter could have achieved. There was another council resolution: this time to erect a "Motor Danger" sign at the corner of Oughtrington Lane and the main road. There was also a national speed limit of 20 mph on all roads in 1912 which remarkably was not lifted until 1930 though it was widely ignored.

Oughtrington Hall - It now forms the core of Lymm High School.

There was no going back. Council records show an increasing number of local businesses seeking permission to store and sell petrol. In 1903 Harry Saville, who had a hardware shop at the Cross, was given a licence to store and sell up to 16 gallons of petrol. By 1905 that had increased to 120 gallons. It is notable too that, when you look at photographs of Lymm from around this time, the subject may be a procession or a farmer displaying his prize horse but in the background signs and hoardings advertising garages or the sale of petrol are regularly starting to appear. By 1909 there is the first mention of a dedicated garage business, Porter & Straker's on Cherry Lane.

In 1911 Henry Ford opened his first factory outside the USA down the road in Trafford Park producing Model T Fords, and mass production was underway. Sales were badly hit by the war though and some of the production capacity was switched to the manufacture of ambulances – up to ten a week at one point. During the war the American entrepreneur poured some of his profits back into an unusual and little known project in Lymm.

In 1914 The Manchester Courier reported:
"Mr Henry Ford the well-known pioneer of The Ford Motors of Detroit USA and Trafford Park Manchester has taken over (by kind permission of Sir W.H.Lever) Oughtrington Hall, Lymm. Mr Ford is equipping and maintaining the same at his own expense and there will be accommodation for 100 Belgian refugees. We understand that it was the original intention of Mr Ford to have wounded soldiers at the hall but this was not possible owing to the fact that Mr Ford is an American citizen."

By 1918 Ford, had spent over $100,000 for the rental of the Oughtrington estate and for the provision of food, shelter, clothing and education.

A Ford mass production car of the 1950s . the Prefect—as seen at Historic Transport Day, There is an identical model on the same stretch of Eagle Brow on the back cover where it is being followed by Ford's two other successes of that time the Anglia and the Popular.

The photographers for these images may have been more interested in the foreground but take a close look at the background too. All of these pictures, taken in the early years of the 20th century, are flagging up the future.

Garage businesses and adverts for petrol were springing up all over the village.

The picture below can be dated precisely. The photograph is inscribed May 20th 1910, the day of the funeral of Edward VII.

Eagle Brow is still surfaced with setts.

Which king are the children asking God to save? Almost certainly George V on the occasion of his Coronation, June 22nd 1911.

Procession Lymm May 20th 1910

This picture of Joseph & Molly Brogdale outside their garage in Mill Lane was taken in the early 50s by Joseph's brother Eric. BP Super was priced at 4/3d a gallon.

At the end of the First World War a young Joseph Brogdale returned to Lymm having served in the army as a driver/mechanic. Looking round to see how he might make a living, he spotted the opportunity to service and maintain cars and so rented space at the Railway Hotel on Mill Lane in what had, until recently, been their stable block. Business was brisk and before long Joseph was able to ask local builder John Holt to construct a purpose built wooden garage almost opposite the pub. By 1925 he was holding 1,000 gallons of petrol. It was around that time that many garages were starting to dispense fuel from hand primed pumps, often situated at the side of the road.

The basic building design was re-used for three more garages in Lymm; Central Garage where the Shell station now stands, Kirkpatricks on Crouchley Lane and Douglas Holt's on Camsley Lane.

By the 1920s the responsibility for major road maintenance finally passed from parish to county authority and the steam rollers were out all over the country laying the revolutionary tarmac that gave major roads a durable weatherproof surface. But amazingly it was not until 1936 that the government recognised that some routes were really national thoroughfares and need to be controlled centrally.

Traffic volumes continued to grow steadily but cars remained the preserve of the middle classes. By 1938 one in fifteen people owned a car in what has been described as "the golden age of motoring". But it was a dangerous business too. Over 120,000 people were killed on Britain's roads between 1918 and 1939. The outbreak of World War Two and the resulting blackout led to chaos and confusion

Wrapped up against the elements for a picnic. These exhibitors at Historic Transport Day are recapturing the spirit of "the golden age of motoring".

A wartime cartoon making light of the blackout—forgive the pun.

on the roads. Within the first couple of days of its introduction John Holt of Camsley Lane had fractured his skull after falling off his motor-bike, and in Warrington two men who were fighting in the road were mown down and killed by a bus that failed to see them. White lines were soon being painted along the kerbs in an attempt to help motorists find their way in the unremitting gloom.

Central Garage on Higher Lane—Today it is the Shell Service Station.

As early as 1914 the government had considered the idea of motorways - or at least *"dedicated routes for motor traffic"* as they called them - and in 1924 a private member's Motorways Bill proposing the construction of major toll roads went before parliament. In 1937 a deputation *"in size and representative character almost without parallel in the history of international relations"* paid a visit to Hitler's Reich to view the new autobahn network. Almost immediately plans were drawn up for England's first toll motorway between London and Birmingham, but war broke out and it was another twenty years before work would start.

By 1957, with the post-war boom in car ownership, several major roads were at full capacity. Traffic volumes were increasing exponentially and in just a couple more years even the AA patrolman on his motorcycle would finally be relieved of the duty to salute every approaching member on the highway. One of the major headaches was the route north over the Ship Canal at Warrington. It was gaining a national reputation as a traffic bottleneck. So when the first stretch of the M6 from Stafford to Preston was given the go-ahead in 1958, it was not surprising that the section that would bypass Warrington was made a top priority.

And so work commenced on what was originally called the Thelwall Bridge but is now universally known as the Thelwall Viaduct. Incidentally the bridge is actually in Lymm but was given its name as it crosses an area called Thelwall Eyes.

By 1935 Lymm was well capable of drumming up an impressive traffic jam like this one at Lymm carnival procession celebrating George V's Silver Jubilee. In the car—provided by the Boumphreys, is Wilhelmina Edwards —"Cotton Queen" for the day.

Our intrepid photographer got into trouble for this one. Rivets were dropping from the sky as he took the picture.

He was probably in a safer place than the other four people in this picture though.

The challenge was to take the biggest road bridge ever built in Britain across five other transport routes: the River Mersey, the Ship Canal, the A56 (formerly the Turnpike Road), the railway and the Bridgewater Canal. The road also had to be built on the soft silt that was the result of deposits from years of dredging the nearby Ship Canal. The main contractors summoned help from American piling experts as they were planning to drive piles down to 170ft to ensure solid foundations. One of the two largest excavators in the world was to be used, but the solution soon threatened to become part of the problem as it sank into the soft earth. Heroic efforts were needed to rescue it and it continued to be used - as a crane!

The start of construction also happened to coincide with the busiest year yet for Ship Canal traffic and building work was not allowed to interrupt the steady flow of shipping traffic.

The opening was originally scheduled for March 1962 but the huge engineering challenge coupled with the longest coldest winter since 1740 put the opening back by sixteen months to July 1963.

Ernest Marples, Transport Minister, was greeted by local dignitaries and representatives of the engineers including Lymm's own Ossie Davies (later Sir Oswald Davies) who had a leading role in the project.

There seems to have been little or no local protest or resistance to this massive new feature on the Lymm landscape, though it had necessitated the destruction of cottages on Camsley Lane. The viaduct was part of the brave new world of motoring of which everyone was clamouring to be a part. This was the age when motorway service cafés were built right next to or above the highway so that customers could admire the traffic. The architects of the bridge also took great pride in the fact that the design had been approved by the Royal Fine Art Commission.

Ossie Davies reported in 1960:

"The viaduct is being pushed steadily ahead. So far it has received minimum publicity. But very soon, when the columns and the crossbeams are up, South West Lancashire and North Cheshire folk will be able to appreciate the shape of things to come and realise that in their midst they will have one of the finest pieces of post war road engineering in Great Britain".

Local people had one day to admire it at close quarters on foot before the opening. The local Rotary club organised a sponsored walk. Also on the bridge that day was an elderly Mrs Winstanley of High Legh - who

"The shape of things to come"

may be the only person ever to have been pushed across the viaduct in a wheelchair! She and her grandson paused as they crossed the Ship Canal and she was able to recall how, as a young girl just over 70 years earlier, she had walked along the bottom of the new Ship Canal the day before it was filled with water.

You can't beat a nice stroll along the M6 on a Sunday afternoon

Traffic growth continued unabated and in 1974 the M56 from Manchester to Chester opened and Lymm found itself at a key motorway crossroads. From being a peaceful backwater Cheshire village, Lymm was now being described by estate agents as " the ideal centre for business travellers" or "superbly located for Manchester Airport and the motorway network." By the early 1990s Thelwall Viaduct was at capacity and had itself become the new bottleneck. An additional viaduct was built which opened in 1995.

Developers clamoured to grab land for new homes partly because Lymm was now so well served by these new fast roads. The village even made the national press as the place with the fastest increasing house prices outside of London. Protests by local groups against the amount of new building, including a car procession through the village to make the point about congestion, met with limited success and there were several major developments around the village.

In the hundred years up to 2011 the population of the village more than doubled from 4,500 to almost 11,000 but, more significantly for the appearance of the village and its environment, the number of homes rose from just 1,100 to over 5,000. Haphazard traffic regulation in the immediate post year wars, which included casual parking around the Cross, was gradually brought under control. By the 1960s the growth in population, the increase in car ownership, and the

proximity of the motorway were all seen as factors contributing to Lymm's growing traffic problems. In 1969 the "no waiting" signs started to go up and it was also the year that Pepper Street opened as the first dedicated car park following the demolition of part of the old school. Later, George Maddox, who had a decorating shop on Church Road, was to recall the day he arrived at his business to see double yellow lines being painted outside. There were demands too for a new bypass to take heavy traffic to the new industrial developments at Carrington and Partington, that came to nothing.

In 1901 there were just a handful of cars in Lymm. By 1951 there were still fewer than 500. Today the figure is way over 5,000 and still growing. Hardly surprising then that traffic and parking continue to pre-occupy local newspapers and residents as they have done for decades during which attempts have been made to fit the proverbial quart into a pint-pot. The problem was solved (for one day at least) in June 2013 when visitors to the village were able to park and ride a vintage bus from the local rugby club into the centre while the hundreds of vintage and classic cars and motor-bikes poured onto the village's May Queen field as part of Lymm's first Historic Transport Day, and enthusiasts had the chance to relive the golden age of motoring.

*This immaculate Aston Martin DB3 was the winner of
the "best in show" award at Historic Transport Day.*

"never too young to enjoy"

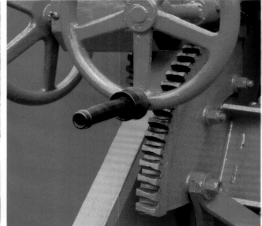

MY 3892

"Delving into Transport History"

Above is the competition winning photograph by
Estelle Cadwallader.

THE SELF-PROPELLED TRAFFIC ASSOCIATION

The canal bridge at New Road is the perfect way to approach the village if the aim is to make a grand entrance. As you stand at the crest, the village is laid out before you. And there have certainly been some memorable sights over the years. In the forties and fifties there was the daily appearance of the coal fired steam wagon of the Alliance Box company, with its firebox blazing, en route from its operation in Partington to premises in Warrington. On an earlier occasion - so Walter Struthers recalled- a steam powered threshing machine came over the bridge in winter and slid slowly down the snow and ice on the village side before burying itself in drifts in front of the Cross where it stayed for several days. But surely the most remarkable and unforgettable visit was on a spring day in 1901 as Lymm was quietly going about its business. The spectacle would have been heard from a long way off before the source of the combined roar of many engines finally crested the Lymm Bridge; a succession of vehicles the like of which the village had never seen. It was the "motoring trial" convoy of the magnificently named Liverpool Self-Propelled Traffic Association.

"The stage-coach is dead and buried, the omnibus is shaken to bits"

Some years previously Alfred Holt, a prominent Liverpool Shipping merchant, had come up with the implausible idea of laying a metal plate-way down the centre of the road from Manchester to Liverpool to carry road based vehicles (at that time still mainly steam driven.) The idea never made it past the drawing board but it did inspire a contingent of local enthusiasts to try to demonstrate that road vehicles were the coming thing as *"the power which will inevitably be"*. The group proclaimed that *"The stage-coach is dead and buried, the omnibus is shaken to bits, and the horse-car is backing to oblivion"*. In order to make their case and also to establish which machines were proving the most successful and robust, they organised trials with an annual drive for three years from Liverpool to Manchester and back via Lymm The test included a timed ascent of Everton Brow for a grand prize of £100 (£7,000 today)

"Lymm was quietly going about its business "–an original sketch of the time by Hedley Fitton

The convoy arrives at Warrington Town Hall shortly after passing through Lymm. There was a crew of three for each "car", a driver, a navigator and a look-out.

They were inspired perhaps by the Rainhill trials over seventy years earlier when Stephenson's Rocket had won the right to haul the first passenger steam service. But there was no contract to be won here, just a group of well to do pioneers on a mission; to spread the word about their vision of the future.

Progress would have been stately on that spring day. While there was an element of competition, at least one of the three man crews recalls especially the pleasure - somewhere between Altrincham and Bowdon - of *" running through a bower of red and white hawthorn, relieved here and there with clusters of laburnum and rhododendron. The breeze was so redolent of its arborescent charges that one felt as though he was rushing through invisible banks of scent."*

After their memorable passage through Lymm the convoy made a stop for lunch at the Patten Arms Hotel in Warrington and the reporter goes on to recount:

"we took up a position in front of the Town Hall at Warrington shortly after one o'clock and a photograph was taken of the novel scene. The proceedings were watched with great interest by a crowd of onlookers. A local committee representing the Warrington Chamber of Commerce and traders of the town and district was present and was greatly interested in the experiment of self-propelled traffic"

By the end of 1902 the association was dissolved following internal disagreements but arguably by then it had fulfilled its mission to show the public – including the people of Lymm – the shape of things to come.

In the same year as Lymm's turnpike road opened, (1824) putting the village on the stage coach route between Manchester and Chester, the next form of public transport was getting under way in Manchester; the omnibus. A horse-drawn service ran three times daily from Pendleton to the city centre. There was no need to book in advance and the carriage would pick up and set down en route though with only nine places there must have been some disappointed potential customers.

The first record of a bus service through Lymm was in 1849 when an enterprising man named George Arnold ran a daily trip leaving the village at 8am in time to connect with the new train service at Altrincham for Manchester at 9am. It stopped to pick up at several pubs along the way including Nag's Head at the top of Eagle Brow, The Jolly Thrasher and The Stamford Arms. There was a return trip in the evening. This service was short-lived though for even as the carriage pulled out of the village each morning work was being completed on the new railway stations at Lymm and Heatley that would open in 1853. Other early horse-drawn bus services were centred on providing excursions such as those run by Mr Connor and Mr

MacGin from Warrington. It was reportedly 1906 before the first Lymm bus service started and it was by all accounts a hair-raising experience. Many years later Mrs Smith of Clay Terrace recalled being persuaded to take one of the first buses to Warrington. She was terrified and wanted to get out and would have preferred to walk.

"They proposed building an electric tramway from Warrington through Lymm to Knutsford"

Things could have been very different if the Ormskirk & Southport Light Electric Railway Company had had their way. In 1899 They proposed building an electric tramway from Warrington through Lymm to Knutsford. The plan was to draw electricity from the new Warrington Electric Power Station but in order for the scheme to be viable they needed permission to lay tramlines within the borough of Warrington. This was not forthcoming. The reason for the objection soon became evident as Warrington submitted its own plans to build a tramway.

This was taken around 1920 . A car and a bus are parked seemingly at random though this spot in front of the Cross was the favoured bus stop for many years.

The photographer's real interest here though was the laying of electrical supply cables. In 1921 there were over 480 authorised suppliers of electricity in England and Wales, who were generating and supplying electricity at a variety of voltages and frequencies.

The lull before the storm. The late 1950s just to the west of Lymm. The picture on the left is Camsley Lane looking towards Warrington. The first cottage on the left was demolished very soon after this picture was taken to make way for the Thelwall Viaduct. The second picture is Warrington Lane almost directly under the path of the motorway.

This opened in 1902 but only as far as Latchford. After some wrangling with the Ship Canal Company who initially demanded what was seen as an exorbitant fee the line extended as far as Stockton Heath but came no nearer to Lymm.

After the First World War there was a rapid expansion in local bus services. Not only was there a huge number of trained drivers returning to their home towns but there was also a glut of vehicles and very little licence control. It was simply a matter of working out a route and giving out handbills to start up. John Wood & Son started operations in Altrincham in 1921 that provided services to Lymm. By 1926 the North West Road Company was running a route from Macclesfield to Lymm and in the late 1930s the number 98 service from Altrincham to Warrington was started and destined to run on that number for nearly 50 years though in 1972 the red of North Western gave way to the green Crossville livery.

Just like the railways some bus routes have disappeared and schedules been reduced with the rise of the motor-car. The main services in and out of the village are now provided by Network Warrington, one of the few bus companies to remain under municipal control.

Historic Transport Day and a ride on the vintage park and ride shuttle is an attraction . The bus is a late 1960s Leyland Leopard.

A RITE OF PASSAGE— "MY FIRST CAR"

For many the dream of owning a car finally became a reality after the Second World War as wages started to rise and prices fell. There was also a growing market in second-hand cars.

The first car was a great rite of passage, particularly for young men who were fascinated by all things mechanical. Notice how two of the owners in these pictures are not just being photographed <u>with</u> their cars. They are in physical contact; such is the pride of ownership.

"The dealer was more like a scrap merchant than a garage"

The car could be vital for work. It was a huge asset for courting and for many the motor car was almost a member of the family. It may even be given a name.

It was 1952 and as a young man of 26 **George Maddox** was setting up his own painting and decorating business. A car and trailer were essential if he was to be able to get to jobs. It was a huge expense but, on a weekly wage of less than £2, George eventually found a 1936 Austin 10 for £120 from a dealer that he described as "more like a scrap merchant than a garage."

There was a lot that didn't work. No speedometer, no fuel gauge, no indica-

tors; but there was no MOT to worry about then. The windscreen washer involved leaning out of the driver's window with a fairy liquid container. And other features that today we take for granted like a heater had not even been introduced. George had his own solution for that. " To keep warm on a cold day I would fill a five gallon metal petrol drum with very hot water and lug it on to the back seat. Sat in the front you could just about feel the heat coming off it."

The car was sixteen years old when George got it but it took him and his wife on plenty of motoring adventures including a trip round the north of Scotland as well as over Hard Knott pass in the Lake District.

George went on to run a successful decorating and hardware shop on Lymm's Church Road for many years and now lives in Grappenhall.

John Gill was one of many who scraped the money together to buy a second-hand motor in the early 60s.

"This was my first car– a 56 Ford Popular. I paid £15-10 shillings for it and four days after buying it my girlfriend (who is now my wife!) and I drove from Lymm up to Aberdeen, before the M6 was built. It was quite a challenge in those days, on the A6 through Preston, Lancaster and up Shap to Scotland; a stay overnight in Carlisle then on to Aberdeenshire.
The car wasn't perfect. It used to jump out of gear in second so one had to hold the gear stick to stop it disengaging. It had a three speed box (no syncromesh) making gear changes slow and noisy.
But looking back after all this time I would love to have another drive of it"

Susan Nash-Eaton was just 18 when she secured a job for the summer as a cook for writer Naomi Mitchison in a remote corner of Kintyre. There were only two problems. She didn't yet have a driving licence and she didn't own a car. Getting there by public transport would be a two day expedition. She passed her test just one day before she was due to set off and her father had bought her a car in anticipation—a Goggomobil. "My father was always attracted to the unusual when it came to buying cars." explained Su.

Goggomobils were produced by a small company in Bavaria that had previously specialised in repairing farm equipment. They had an unenviable reputation for being extremely unreliable.

"I made it to Carradale but when I look at my diary of the Summer of '62 every day seemed to involve a trip to the garage or being towed back from somewhere."

Su is seen here busy on the daily repairs. **Su Williams**, as she is now, lives in the village at Leckonby Cottage.

Su—busy on her daily running repairs.

And finally .. From the ridiculous to the sublime. There aren't many people who can claim a Roll-Royce as their first car. For **Roger Nowell** it was a "first" in a different sense as he explains ..

"It would be fair to say that old Rolls-Royces are in my blood. ANA 21 started life in Whitefield in Manchester in 1933, moved to Ulverston, Cumbria in the early fifties and was purchased by my late father in 1958 and used as the main family car until 1972 when it was taken off the

road due to poor condition. I was brought home in the car as a new-born baby in 1964 and remember as a child, family summer holidays in Cornwall with suitcases and bicycles strapped to the rear. It was very little used from 1972 until restoration started in 2008

AYU 884 was delivered new in 1934 to a Surgeon in Harley Street, London . Next owner was a Reverend in Somerset , then a consultant anaesthetist in Bristol and

finally my late father in 1966. After constant use and in very tired condition, it was broken up for scrap in 1966 though the parts were never actually disposed of and were kept together until restoration commenced some thirty years later in 1996. A process that took an initial five years then a further ten years as a rolling restoration. This car is a unique body design and is the only one in existence."

By the way this may be the only book ever to feature images of a Goggomobil and a Rolls on the same page!

Alan Taylor was born in Lymm and has never left. He lives today on Dairy Farm Close with his wife Eileen.

"When I left school in 1953 I started work at Millings, the Grocers, where Baci's restaurant is now. I worked in the shop and went out on van deliveries. That is where I had my first driving lessons, thanks to Harold, Old Bill, and Long John. I had a provisional licence and a set of L plates. No-one apart from me and the drivers knew I was driving without insurance. The roads around High Legh were a learner's paradise as they were so quiet and almost traffic free.

The vans were one and half and one ton Austin Commercials. They were very noisy with long floppy gear levers.

Harold taught me to change gear without using the clutch by judging the engine revs. Obviously I could not use these to take a driving test so I booked four lessons with the local driving instructor, a Mr.Pooley, who had an old three gear Ford Popular.

After passing my test I saved up to buy my first car. A Morris Minor, series 2, was advertised locally by Mr. Caldwell and I took it for a test drive. After driving the vans, and the Ford Popular, it felt as nippy as a sports car. It cost me in the region of £180. The first petrol I bought was from Sam Wright's Garage on Rush Green and I paid 4/6d per gallon. That car was my pride and joy and it was the first car owned by anyone in my family!

A few years ago I realised that I had a photograph of my car taken two years before I bought it. It had been parked outside the Spread Eagle (see picture on back cover WMB 639) so clearly it was meant to be mine one day.

Driving opened up so many wonderful opportunities. It changed my whole way of life. I drove to the Lake District, a three hour trip each way, and when I saw the

The shop where Alan worked and the van on which he learnt to drive. One of his other duties was to build the pyramid can displays.

Langdale Pikes, I realised I wanted to be up there. I was bitten by the climbing bug. For a shy local lad from Lymm it brought a whole new dimension into my life. Trips to Wales and Scotland soon followed.

The car saw me through marriage and fatherhood. It was eventually sold to a young lad in Statham and it was his first car as well".

LEFT: A first look at the Langdales thanks to the freedom of the road . There is no-one about and the view in the background is not too bad ; but just take a look at my new car !

PUTTING THE "SPORT" IN TRANSPORT

For many people simply owning a motor vehicle in the 50s was enough but for a growing band of enthusiasts their transport was also their passion . By the age of 20 **Michael Brogdale** had already owned a couple of bikes but in 1954 he read about BSA's new model—the 497cc Shooting Star and having just completed his engineering apprenticeship he put his name down for one—due for delivery the following spring for the princely sum of £238.

Somehow the local dealer managed to get hold of six early bikes—most were heading for export —and Michael got the first one, making him an instant biking celebrity among local riders. It was to be the start of a sixty year relationship that continues to this day.

His first instinct was adventure and foreign trips quickly followed; to Spain, Switzerland and Austria and then in 1959, with wife June, to Norway. " It was all dirt roads once we got out of town" explained Michael "but the scenery was stunning and we would ride for miles without seeing another vehicle. The scariest part was probably the new tunnels that were barely lit in those days."

"a crash on the finishing line at Silverstone"

Display shelves with over sixty trophies testify to many years of racing that culminated in his becoming production bike club champion in the mid 60s, still on the Shooting Star. (See pictures top and bottom) Michael's racing career was rudely interrupted in 1966 by a crash on the finishing line at Silverstone when he suffered extensive facial injuries.   He was judged to have crossed the line though, if unconventionally, and was awarded second place.

It wasn't too long before he was "back in the saddle" and so Michael, a lifelong resident of Lymm, continued to enjoy his passion for motor sport—still on the same bike, progressively tuned up and refined over many years, until the age of 75.

Now 80 Michael still likes to get out around the Cheshire lanes on a sunny afternoon. " I can't imagine not riding" said Michael " the bike is so old now that it is exempt from both and MOT and tax, and anyway I paid £238 for it so I want to make sure I get my money's worth out of it !"

ONE MAN'S JOURNEY FROM BY-WAY TO HIGHWAY

Sir Oswald "Ossie" Davies

Among the many small food and produce retailers in Lymm who traded with horse and cart in the early years of the twentieth century was George Warham Davies. His business used to take him round the neighbourhood including Camsley Lane on the road to Warrington. As the years went by he must have encountered the first cars or buses along the way. But it would have been difficult for him to imagine that within fifty years there would be a six lane highway soaring above the countryside. If you had also told him that one of his children would mastermind that great construction project he would likely have shaken his head in disbelief.

Oswald Davies (or "Ossie" as he always preferred to be called) was born in 1920 into a large family in Heatley, the seventh of ten children. He was a bright lad who showed plenty of initiative. He was educated at Central School, Sale to which he won a scholarship. At the age of fifteen Ossie took a short walk from home that was to set the course of his life. Nearby on Mill Lane, a small building contractor, Leonard Fairclough, was laying a sewer. Ossie stood and watched for a few minutes before summoning the nerve to ask if there was any work going. He was hired as tea boy for what was supposed to be a holiday job. However the site agent soon realised that he had a

bright lad on his hands and took him under his wing, giving him clerical work, surveying, engineering and other tasks. Night school studies followed and by the young age of nineteen the "tea boy" had his first assignment as agent in charge of a site in Ulverston.

The war interrupted his meteoric rise through the company. Ossie joined the Royal Engineers where he volunteered to work in bomb disposal and also qualified as a diver. His bravery brought him a Distinguished Conduct Medal and he was described by his C.O. as "an exemplary Warrant Officer and an inspiration to the men under his command."

Almost there ...

The pony and trap on the Thelwall Viaduct may have been partly Ossie's idea but he is not in the picture; he is taking it. That is his son Neville on the left who still lives in the village. On the right is Sir James Drake a civil engineer who was regarded as a leading pioneer of the national motorway network.

That experience of leadership was to prove invaluable when he returned to Fairclough's and within three years he was a director of a rapidly expanding company. The 1960s produced a huge increase in road building focused on the growing motorway network. Fairclough's joined a consortium with Alfred McAlpine to build the Warrington to Preston section of the M6. Following the success of this huge project, which included the building of the Thelwall Viaduct, Ossie became chair of the group in 1965 and later chair of the AMEC group.

Lymm remained Ossie's home throughout his career where he lived with his wife Joyce and two children. So it would have been a matter of particular local pride to him to be at the helm of the Thelwall Viaduct project. He devoted much of his energies to the community. He was a councillor for twenty years and an active Rotarian. He came to the financial rescue of Warrington Rugby League Club culminating in his leading them onto the pitch at Wembley in the 1974 cup final. He also instigated the building of Lymm Youth & Community Centre.

In 1984 "Ossie" became Sir Oswald.

To mark the opening of the viaduct in a unique way, Ossie and his son came up with the idea of riding over it in a pony and trap. Son, Neville, was despatched to Smart's of Appleton to collect the trap, and at 6am on a Summer's morning in 1963 they climbed the incline of the huge new bridge to take in the view. They may well have paused to look down on Camsley Lane where Ossie's father once plied his trade and pondered just how quickly the world can turn in fifty years.

Back to the Future

A VILLAGE AT THE CROSSROADS

AT THE TIME OF WRITING [2013] **TWO MASSIVE INFRASTRUCTURE PROJECTS** of national significance are being proposed that would both have a direct impact on Lymm. Remarkably, if both are carried out, they will intersect at the village of Warburton just a mile to the east of the village.

The Atlantic Gateway is a proposed redevelopment strategy for the North West of England. It is potentially a £50bn investment over 50 years, and is led by Peel Holdings. It centres on a regeneration of the Mersey ports and a massively increased use of the Ship Canal Already in the last few years some cargoes have started to move back onto the canal, including wines for Tesco and cereals for Kelloggs as road transport becomes ever more expensive and more congested.

When the Ship Canal was first built, the primary aim was to turn Manchester into a major port and, in so doing, by-pass Liverpool. Since then, ocean-going container ships have increased massively in size. Even the Panama Canal has had to be widened to cope. In the new development Liverpool and Birkenhead will become world shipping hubs with goods being trans-shipped onto smaller vessels for dispersal including along the Ship Canal.

The plan has, not surprisingly, re-awakened the old rivalry between Liverpool and Manchester with each city keeping an eagle eye on the other as plans unfold.

The vision is not without its local critics too. Residents in the area are questioning the impact of the huge increase in levels of canal traffic. Much has changed since the canal was first built. Very many more people live along its banks. The amount of road traffic has also increased massively , and the two forms of transport interact wherever one has to cross the other. The first swing-bridges crossing the Ship Canal were built at a time when the horse and the bicycle provided the only land based transport. Now, however, there is concern at the potential for local traffic chaos.

But it is HS2, the proposed new north-south high-speed rail line, which is currently preoccupying the national news and many local people.

The argument for the line is that it is considered to be essential to provide increased capacity and will also offering high speed journeys. It is claimed that it will bring greater prosperity for the region.

Phase 2 of this project (the section north of Birmingham) is out for consultation and has met with fierce local opposition along the whole route. The line would run just to the east of Lymm on a route north from the A50 near the Mere Court Hotel, where there would then be a large junction for a spur to Manchester Airport and the city centre. The main line towards

Transport issues provoke strong local interest and reaction. 150 people packed the Community Centre for a debate about HS2 in September 2013. The overwhelming feeling of the meeting was opposition.

Wigan would cross the A56 between Agden and the Old No 3 pub in Little Bollington and would rise on a similar scale to the Thelwall Viaduct to span the Ship

Canal just east of Warburton Bridge. Many properties would be demolished to make away for the line and others complain that their homes are already "blighted" since the proposed route was announced.

Local members of the STOP HS2 campaign caused a few turned heads in Lymm on a Saturday night with their "It's a White Elephant" campaign

Local politicians too are sceptical about the benefits for the Warrington area whilst also being concerned about the environmental cost and the effect on people's lives. In October 2013 Warrington council leader Terry O'Neill expressed concern about unnecessary disruption and loss of jobs at Taylor Business Park in Culcheth with no compensating economic benefit.

At the moment the government is standing firm but there appears to be increasing unrest in all the main political parties about whether HS2 is the right solution and the best way of spending a huge sum of money - currently the budget is over £40bn.

POPLARS TRANSPORT HERITAGE CENTRE

Here is another view of the future. This one is looking back from 2063

Opened ten years ago in 2053 on the site of the abandoned Truck Stop the centre celebrates the nation's love affair with the motor car that lasted nearly one hundred and fifty years during the period that is now often referred to as "the great fossil fuel fest". It is hard to believe looking back that as recently as the end of the last century a new Thelwall Viaduct had to be built to accommodate the extra traffic generated by universal car ownership and road-based commerce.

Today of course since the introduction of personal mileage allowances and the vast improvements in face to face 3D video contacts, not to mention home working legislation, domestic car use has returned to levels last seen a hundred years ago. This has led to one of the viaducts becoming redundant as a road enabling it to become part of the "north-south divide" eco-trail for bicycles, solar scooters and walkers. As you stroll across don't miss the viewing platform at the highest point from where you can see a whole history of transport rolling out before you. Starting from the south we see what was originally the turnpike road, later known as the A56, - and now home to the super-tram service from Warrington to Altrincham, or "Waltr" as it is affectionately known. Next to it is the much loved Trans-Pennine trail , a vital link for our

One of the very early American solar scooters from 2005. Just one of the many historical exhibits at the Transport Heritage Centre.

modern day "scoota-commutas". Above it and oldest of all is the Bridgewater Canal. If you arrive at the right time of day you may see the shuttle boat passing through taking students from their halls of residence at the old Lymm Hotel to Grappenhall University College. And finally there is the Manchester Ship Canal — a busy hive of commercial activity once more but also home to countless cruise ships full of Chinese tourists en route to visit the "Cotton Experience" and the "Museum of the Internet" in Manchester.

Use the telescope to look a little further east to where you can trace a line of pillars that were to form part of something called the "HS2 north-south rail-link". This was abandoned of course by the Labour – Green coalition government in 2025 by which time costs had reached £200 billion against a backdrop of falling business and domestic travel. The remaining pillars are known locally as "Osborne's Obelisks".

Back at the Heritage Centre there is plenty to do.

Visitor Centre entrance - faithfully reconstructed from the original .

 Find out what it was like to stay overnight in the cab of your own lorry watching endless repeats of Top Gear (This programme was popular over fifty years ago with transport lovers who were known as "petrolheads". It was finally withdrawn by the BBC with a formal apology in 2020). Or you could experience traffic chaos at first hand in the "jam simulator". People today find it hard to believe that in the early twenty-first century drivers on the Thelwall Viaduct were often travelling more slowly than the pleasure boats below them. We'll pump non-toxic fumes into your simulator pod whilst playing you cheery Radio 2 traffic reports to re-create the whole weekend away experience for you.

And before you leave jump aboard one of our vintage Austin Allegros or BMWs for a ride on the Big-Mac Drive Thru. But don't worry. It's just for fun. You don't have to eat it. Just throw the packaging out of the window. This seems to have been a local tradition at the time. Instead you can enjoy a healthy snack on the very site of the original driver's restaurant eating locally sourced bacon, eggs and beans. And why not swill it down with a glass of High Legh Sauvignon Blanc. After all you're not driving !

If you've not come by solar scooter then make sure you don't miss the last Supertram home at 23.40.

Have a great day.

Homeward Bound on the heritage trail - Bicycle, Canal and Motorway

Lymm Cross 1950s

Acknowledgements

This has been a first book for both of us so we simply wouldn't have got there without the help of a great number of people who not only had the knowledge but also the patience and generosity to guide us through the whole process. They are Jim Williams for his tactful and fastidious editing, Kerry Knight who dotted our i's and crossed our t's as proof-reader, Joe Griffiths and Lymm & District Local History Society who shared their knowledge, stories and picture collection, Derron, Glenda and Moya at W.G. Bairds, our printers, who have been patience personified and have led us through the tricky stuff, Lymm Photographic Society with special mention to Carol Sparkes and Bill Rigby firstly for taking all those pictures on Transport Day and secondly for sharing them with us, Gill Fox who has chronicled so many village events, Colin Grimes for creating our village transport map, the staff at Warrington Library. We also need to thank all those people who have shared pictures and reminiscences and given us their time including Michael Brogdale, Jeanne Artingstall, John Gill, George Maddox, Su Williams, Mimi Alderman, Cyril Wood , Neville Davies and Roger Nowell. There have been many others and organisations whose names appear in the credits who have allowed us to use pictures. Thanks to them also. And finally to our wives who have indulged us while we sat staring endlessly at computer screens.

Bibliography

Transport Revolution from 1770 (Studies in Economic & Social History) Philip Bagwell 1974

The Minutes Tell the Story Lymm 1895-1974
 (Lymm & District Local History Society) G.H. Thomas

Lymm & District Local History leaflet collection of personal reminiscences .

Websites.

http://thinkingaboutcycling.wordpress.com/social-movements-and-the-bicycle
Insights into the social history of cycling.

http://www.canalscape.net/ (author Cyril J. Wood) for a more detailed history of Manchester Ship Canal, The Bridgewater Canal and Lymm Cruising Club

http://www.steamershistorical.co.uk/steamers_bridgewater_tugs.htm
Interesting collection of images of early steam tugs – including the *Lymm*

http://www.britishnewspaperarchive.co.uk/
Great access to countless local stories over the past 250 years.

Picture Credits —with thanks

Introduction
8 Alan Taylor

The Age of Horsepower
10 (both) Alan Taylor Collection
11 Alan Taylor Collection
12 (top) L&DHS
12 (bottom) BNA
13 Alan Taylor via Maurice Cadman
14 (both) Alan Taylor Collection
15 (both) Alan Taylor Collection
16 (top right) Carol Sparkes
16 (left) BNA
17 Michael Brogdale

The Most Extraordinary Thing
18 Gill Fox
19 (all) Alan Taylor
20 (L&DHS)
21 (top) BNA
21 (bottom) Alan Taylor
22 Alan Taylor Collection
23 (top) BNA
23 Alan Taylor Collection
24 L&DHS
25 (top) Michael Brogdale
25 (bottom) Alan Williams
26 Cyril Wood Collection
27 Alan Taylor (both)
28 (top) Cyril Wood Collection
28 (bottom) Alan Taylor Collection
29 Lymm Cruising Club
30 (both) Carol Sparkes
31 (top left) M & R Alderman
31 (top right) Gill Fox
31 (bottom left) Bill Rigby
31 (bottom right) Gill Fox
32 (top) Gill Fox
32 (bottom left) Gill Fox
32 (bottom right) Chris Moore
33 (top) Alan Taylor
33 (bottom) Carol Sparkes
34 (left) Carol Sparkes
34 (top right) M & R Alderman
34 (centre right) Gill Fox
34 (bottom right) Gill Fox
35 Cherie Brown
36 Alan Taylor Collection
36 (bottom) Alan Taylor
37 (top) GMCRO
37 (bottom) Alan Taylor Collection
38 Alan Taylor Collection

38 Alan Taylor
39 Alan Taylor

Turnpikes and Toll Bridges
40 Alan Taylor
41 (left) Alan Taylor
41 (right) Warrington Library
42 Alan Taylor Collection
43 (left) L&DHS
43 (bottom) Alan Taylor Collection
44 (left) Cyril Wood
44 (right) L&DHS
45 (all) Alan Taylor
46 (left) L&DHS
46 (right) BNA
47 Gill Fox

The Steam Age
48 (top) Alan Taylor
48 (bottom) BNA
49 L&DHS
50 (left) Don & Joyce Smith
50 Alan Williams Collection
51 (right) Don & Joyce Smith
51 (left) Alan Taylor Collection
52 Alan Taylor via Walter Struthers
52 (bottom) BNA
53 Michael Stewart
54 (left) Alan Taylor Collection
54 (right) BNA
55 (both) L&DHS
56 H.B. Priestley via Paul Wright
57 (top) David Ingham
57 (bottom) Andrew Salmon
58 (top) BNA
58 (bottom) L&DHS
59 Alan Taylor Collection
60 (top) Family of Roy Holt
60 (bottom) Lachlan Main
60 ticket Michael Stewart
61 unknown
61 (bottom) Michael Brogdale
62 (top) Michael Stewart
62 (centre) John Gill
62 (bottom) Alan Taylor
62 (ticket) – Michael Stewart
63 (both) Alan Taylor Collection
64 (top) Warrington Model Railway Club
64 (bottom) wiki-images
65 (all) Carol Sparkes

Ships across the Fields
66 Alan Taylor
67 (top) Alan Taylor Collection
67 (bottom) GMCRO
68 Alan Taylor
69 GMCRO
70 (top) GMCRO
70 (bottom) Alan Williams Collection
71 Cyril wood
72 (both) Alan Taylor Collection
73 (top) Alan Taylor Collection
73 (bottom) BNA
74 Alan Taylor
75 Alan Taylor
76 Alan Williams
77 L&DHS

Pedalling History
78 David Taylor
79 (both) L&DHS
80 (both) Bolton Clarion Club
81 (left) L&DHS
81 (other two) Alan Taylor
82 (top) Des Hawley
82 (bottom) Veteran Cycle Club
83 (left-top&bottom) Carol Sparkes
83 (three pics right) Veteran Cycle
84 Hedley Fitton
85 Hedley Fitton
86 Hedley Fitton
87 (left) Anthony O'Neil (Geograph)
87 (top right) – unknown
87 (bottom) Bolton Clarion Club

That Intolerable Nuisance
88 L&DHS
89 (left) unknown
89 (Rtght) L&DHS
90 L&DHS
91 (top left) Alan Taylor Collection
91 (bottom right) Gill Fox
92 (Top left) Alan Taylor Collection
92 (b'm left) Alan Taylor Collection
92 (right) David Taylor
93 Michael Brogdale
94 (top right) Helen Kulczycki
94 (right) unknown
94 (bottom left) L&DHS
95 Alan Taylor Collection
96 (both) Alan Taylor
97 (top) Alan Taylor
97 (bottom) Neville Davies

98/99 Alan Taylor
100 (all) Bill Rigby
101 (top pair) Cherie Brown
101 (bottom left) Helen Kulczycki
101 (bottom right) Stephen Bell
102 (top left) Helen Kulczycki
102 (top right) Cherie Brown
102 (centre left) Helen Kulczycki
102 (centre right) Carol Sparkes
102 (bottom left) Carol Sparkes
102 (bottom right) Carol Sparkes
103 (top left) Carol Sparkes
103 (top right) George Dutton
103 (centre left) Gill Fox
103 (centre) Geoff Statham
103 (centre right) Gill Fox
103 (bottom left) Gill Fox
103 (bottom right) Carol Sparkes
104 (top left) Gill Fox
104 (top right) Gill Fox
104 (bottom left) Gill Fox
104 (bottom right) Helen Kulczycki
105 (top) Estelle Cadwallader
105 (bottom left) Bill Rigby
105 (bottom centre) Cherie Brown
105 (bottom right) Cherie Brown
106 (left) Hedley Fitton
106 (right) unknown
107 Liverpool Motor Club
108 L&DHS
109 (top pair) Alan Taylor
109 (bottom) Cherie Brown
110 (centre column) George Maddox
110 (right) John Gill
111 (left) Su Williams
111 (other three) Roger Nowell
112 (both) Alan Taylor
113 (top and bottom) Michael Brogdale
113 (centre) Alan Taylor
114 (top) Neville Davies
114 (bottom) Alan Taylor
115 Neville Davies

Back to the Future
116 Alan Williams
117 (right) Rebecca Bennett
117 (left) Alan Williams
118 Don Dunklee
119 (left) Alan Williams
119 (right) James McCollom
120 Alan Taylor

L&DHS = Lymm & District History Society   BNA = British Newspaper Archive   GMCRO = Courtesy of Greater Manchester County Record Office

About the authors ...

Alan Williams is new to Lymm. He has only lived here for twenty years. Alan's introduction to Lymm's fascinating history was through the making of two videos, The Lymm Film (2000) and The Winter's Tale (2001). Since retiring in 2011 Alan has been involved with a number of village activities including forming The Big Sing choir and creating the first Lymm Historic Transport Day in June 2013. Alan lives with his wife Su in a Norwegian log house by the canal and, when he has time, likes to make music.

Alan Taylor is a Lymm Grey (see page 10). He was born in a cottage by the Bridgewater Canal. His father was a boatman on the Ship Canal taking young Alan on many trips. After discovering photography at the age of 15 and working locally as a grocer and then a butcher he began a career as a press photographer. Before retiring in 2003 he was Chief Photographer for a local newspaper group in mid and south Cheshire, being in the enviable position of having combined his job with his hobby. Alan lives in Dairy Farm Close with his wife, Eileen.

Supporting Community Events

A donation of £3 per copy for the first 1,000 copies sold will be made to the Lymm Historic Transport Day Group to help secure the financial future of transport events in the village. For more information about this event and about the book and also to order more copies go to www.lymmtransport.org.uk. If you have images or stories about Lymm that you would like to share for possible inclusion in a future book we would love to hear from you.
Alan Williams 01925-754080 alanlymm@gmail.com

The Big Picture (next page)

A highlight of Lymm Festival Foodfest June 20th 2013 was the unveiling of the annual BIG PICTURE.
Managed by Lymm Festival and painted in sixty panels by local artists the image is based on "The Opening of the Bridgewater Canal 1761" by Ford Madox Brown. The original, completed in 1892, is number eleven in a series of twelve murals that are on permanent display in Manchester Town Hall.

The picture caused quite a furore when it was unveiled. Brown made the users of the canal his foreground heroes. The Duke, Brindley and his entourage were relegated to the background.

Twin babies are tied to a boat and are waving blue flags but not even looking at the ceremony. There is a even a small dog struggling to get out of the water to the left indicating the generally chaotic nature of the ceremony.

Councillors were so perturbed by the image that they demanded to see a sketch of his final mural in the series of twelve before allowing him to go ahead.

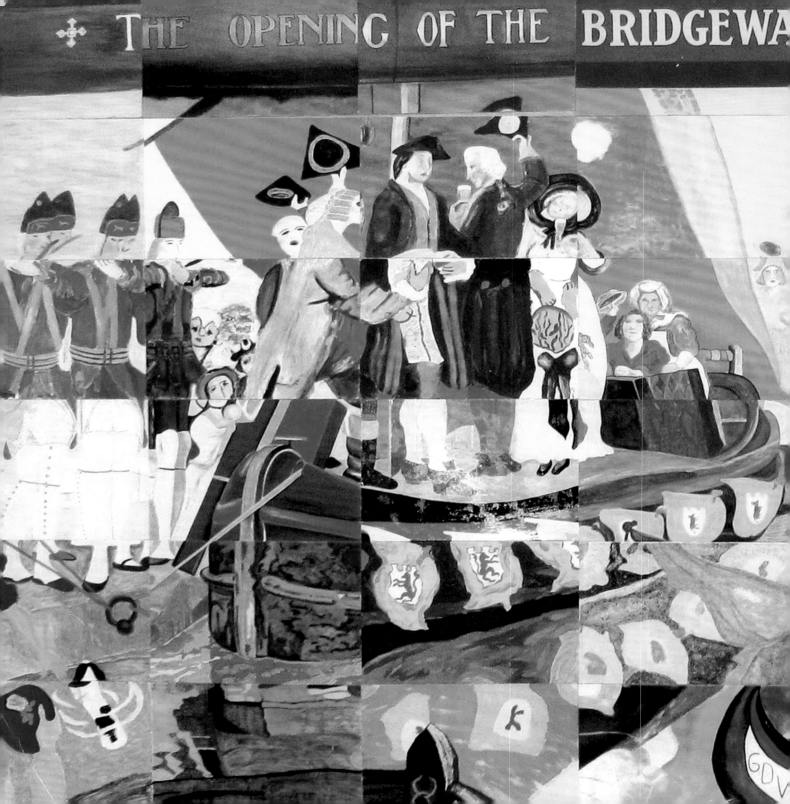